METAPHYSICALLY
Speaking

The Bible is the greatest How-To book ever written

Rev. Dr. Della Reese Lett

Lett/Reese International Publishing Co.

PREFACE

My teacher Dr. Johnnie Colemon who was also my mentor, often said "It works if you work it." I have found that to be the truth. Studying with her, I learned to go beyond the top stories (the allegories) of the Bible, to the metaphysical meanings.

Beyond the physical, to the depth of the functional use of the allegories, which were written for us to be able to live the peace-filled, joyous, prosperous, understanding and functional life of one made in the image-likeness of our Father God. The reason God sent His son Jesus Christ, our Wayshower, with instructions was to establish the right attitudes in us.

This book is filled with the lessons and materials that I give to my congregation at Understanding Principles for Better Living Church in Los Angeles, CA. I was not then, nor am I now concerned with winning a grammar contest. But, it is very important to me that you get this information. So, I have written it the same way I speak it.

I have learned and now live in the magnificence of God. And I want to share what I have learned with you so that you too can see what Jesus and the Dr.'s Colemon, Fillmore, Cady, Fox, Lamsa, Goldsmith and many others have written for us to help us along our way in accepting "it works if you work it." You will know when you are "working it" for you will begin reaping the benefits God intended for us.

I would like to be a part of that.

METAPHYSICALLY SPEAKING

Affirmations

A Metaphysical Understanding

I remind the people I pastor on a regular basis that we are a part of a teaching ministry. We teach the teachings of Jesus.

Metaphysical = beyond physics, beyond the surface to the depth, the real meanings of the teachings.

We offer a series of tools by which you can reach a true understanding of The Word, making you better able, through understanding, to apply the principles provided for you by our Father God, His Son Jesus and the power of the Holy Spirit; the whole Spirit of God.

One of those tools is called the "Metaphysical Dictionary".

It is a very important tool because all of the names in the Bible, names of towns, people, situations and incidents have a deeper meaning than the allegory in which they are presented.

During Jesus' time and for years after, one could be killed for being a Christian and so people had to speak to each other in a coded manner for their safety.

Let us begin by studying thinking. I want to investigate with you, the first recorded miracle of Jesus.

1

A METAPHYSICAL UNDERSTANDING

John 2:1-11 *"And the third day there was a marriage in Cana of Galilee; and the mother of Jesus was there;*

And both Jesus was called and His disciples, to the marriage.

And when they wanted wine, the mother of Jesus said unto Him, 'They have no wine.'

Jesus said unto her, 'Woman, what have I to do with thee? Mine hour is not yet come.'

His mother said unto the servants, 'Whatsoever He says to you do it!'"

And there were set there six waterpots of stone, after the manner of the purifying of the Jews, containing two or three firkins apiece.

Jesus said, 'Fill the waterpots with water.' And they filled them up to the brim. And He said unto them "Draw out now, and bear unto the governor of the feast.' And they bear it.

When the ruler of the feast tasted the water that was made wine, and knew not from whence it was: but the servants which drew the water knew; the governor of the feast called the bridegroom.

Every man at the beginning doth set forth good wine; and when men have well drunk, then that wine which is worse; but thou hast kept the good wine until now."

This beginning of miracles Jesus did in Cana of Galilee and manifested forth His glory; and His disciples believed on Him.

We are going to give up completely the idea that this is just another story, maybe historical, but certainly having nothing to do with us, and our way of living today.

Wrong! Wrong! Wrong!

We are going to capture the spiritual, mental, and scientific view of the laws of the mind, which Jesus was teaching us.

"And the third day there was a marriage in Cana of Galilee and the mother of Jesus was there."

Galilee means your mind or your consciousness.

Cana means your desire.

The marriage is purely mental or the subjective embodiment of your desire.

This whole beautiful drama of prayer is a psychological one in which all the characters are mental states, feelings and ideas within you, me - us.

One of the many meanings of Jesus is illumined reason.

The mother of Jesus means the feeling, moods, or emotions, which possess us.

"And both Jesus was called, and His disciples, to the marriage."

Your disciples are your inner powers and faculties enabling you to realize your desires.

And when they wanted wine, the mother of Jesus saith unto Him, "They have no wine."

Wine represents the answered prayer or the manifestation of your desire and ideals in life.

Now let's put this into perspective so you can see that this is an everyday drama taking place in our own lives.

When we wish to accomplish something, be it supply, a way out of your problems, increasing finances, solving relationship problems, whatever, suggestions of lack come to you, such as, "There is no hope," or "All is lost," or "I can't accomplish this, it's hopeless." This is the voice from the outside world saying to you, "They have no wine," or "look at the facts." This is your feeling of lack, limitation, or bondage talking to you.

Okay, I got that part Rev.. Della, how do I meet these challenges of circumstances and conditions?

We claim victory with the laws of the mind, with thinking.

Another tool is the affirmation.

As I think and feel inside, so is my outside world; my body, finances, environment, social position, and all the phases of my external relationship to the world and mankind.

Our internal, mental movements and imagery govern, control and direct the external plan of our lives.

The Bible says, *"As a man thinkest in his heart so is he."*

The heart is a "Chaldean word" meaning the subconscious mind.

Our thoughts must reach subjective subconscious levels by engaging the power of our subliminal self.

The subliminal self is the self below the consciousness perception.

A METAPHYSICAL UNDERSTANDING

Thoughts and feelings are our destiny. Thought charged with feeling and interest are always subjectified and becomes manifest in your world.

Prayer is a marriage of thought and feeling, or your ideas and emotions; this is what the marriage feast represents.

Any, get this word, **any** idea or desire of the mind, felt as true comes to pass, whether it is good, bad, or indifferent. Knowing the law now, that what you imagine and feel in your mind, you will express, manifest, or experience in the outside, enables you to begin to discipline your mind. Huh?

When suggestions of lack, fear, doubt, or despair ("they have no wine") come to your mind, immediately reject it mentally by focusing your attention at once on the answered prayer, or the fulfillment of your desire.

The statements, *"Mine hour is not yet come,"* and *"Woman what have I to do with thee"* are figurative, idiomatic, oriental expressions.

Woman means the negative feeling that you indulge in. These negative suggestions have no power or reality.

Because there is nothing to back them up!

A suggestion of lack has no power; the power resides in your own thoughts and feelings.

What does God mean to you? Here we are again. What does God mean to you?

God is the one invisible source from which all things flow.

5

A METAPHYSICAL UNDERSTANDING

When our thoughts are constructive and harmonious, the spiritual power, being responsive to our thought, flows as harmony, health, and abundance.

We have to practice the discipline of completely rejecting every thought of lack by immediately recognizing the availability of the spiritual power, and its response to our constructive thoughts and imagery.

Then you will be practicing the truth found in these words, woman (in this case represents negativity) *"What have I to do with thee?"*

"Mine hour is not yet to come."

While you have not yet reached a conviction or positive state of mind, you know you are on the way mentally, because you are engaging your mind on positive ideals, goals, and objectives in life.

Whatever our minds dwell upon, it multiplies, magnifies, and causes it to grow until finally the mind becomes qualified with the new state of consciousness.

Then we are conditioned positively, whereas before we were conditioned negatively.

The spiritual man/woman, with the use of prayer, moves from the mood of lack to the mood of confidence, peace and trust in the spiritual power within himself/herself.

When our trust and faith are in the spiritual power, the mother (moods and feelings) registers a feeling of triumph or victory; this is what brings about the solution or the answer to our prayer.

The water pots = the mental cycles that we go through in order to bring about the subjective realization of our desires.

6

The length of time may be a moment, an hour, a week, or a month, depending on our faith and state of consciousness.

In prayer we must cleanse our mind of false belief, fear, doubt, and anxiety by becoming completely detached from our senses and the external world.

Why?

John 17:16-17 *"They are not of the world even as I am not of the world. Sanctify them through thy truth: thy word is truth."*

John 8:23 *"Ye are from beneath; I am from above: ye are of this world; I am not of this world."*

The methods of the world will not work for us because we are following our Wayshower Jesus, who is not of this world, so we are not of this world. So we must...

John 7:24 *"Judge not according to the appearance, but judge the righteous judgment."*

The righteous judgment is right thinking, followed by right actions. We have need to meditate on the joy of the answered prayer until that inner certitude comes, whereby you know that you know what you know.

Mark 9:23 *"If thou canst believe, all things are possible to him that believes."*

Mark 11:24 *"Therefore I say unto you, what things so ever you desire when you pray, believe that you receive them, and you shall have them."*

When you have succeeded in being one with your desire, you have succeeded in the mental marriage or the union of your feelings with your idea.

7

Every time we pray we are trying to perform the marriage feast of Cana (the realization of your desire or ideals).

John 2:7 *"They filled them up to the brim"*

The six waterpots represent our own minds in the spiritual and mental creative act.

We must fill our minds to the brim, meaning we must become filled full, of the feeling of being, and having, what you long to be or desire to have.

When you succeed in filling your mind with the idea you wish to accomplish or express, you are full to the brim. Then you cease praying about it; for you feel its reality in your mind.

You know, that you know what you know, and you know that what you know is truth and cannot fail.

John 2:8 *"And He said to them, "Draw out now, and bear unto the governor of the feast."*

You are always governing your mental feast. You must reject the unfit for mental consumption thoughts, suggestions, opinions, sights and sounds that reach your eyes and ears during the day, sometimes, most times, thousands of times a day.

You are the only one that can control your thinking.

Your conscious, reasoning, intellectual mind is the governor of the feast.

When you consciously choose to entertain, meditate, feast upon and imagine your heart's desire as true, it becomes a living embodiment and a part of your mentality, so that your deeper self, gives birth or expression to it.

In other words, what is impressed subjectively is expressed objectively.

John 2:9 *"When the ruler of the feast tasted the water that was made wine, and knew not from whence it was: but the servants which drew the water knew; the governor of the feast called the bridegroom."*

Water represents the invisible, formless, spiritual power, unconditioned consciousness.

Wine is conditioned consciousness, or the mind giving birth to its beliefs and convictions.

The servants, who draw the water for you represent the mood of peace, confidence, and faith.

According to your faith or feeling, your good is attracted or drawn to you.

So this is not just a nice story.

In the first recorded miracle of Jesus, we are told that prayer is a marriage feast, or the mind uniting with its desire.

Love is the fulfilling of the law. Love is really an emotional attachment, a sense of oneness with your good.

You must be true to that which you love.

You must be loyal to your purpose or to your ideal.

We are not being true to the one we love, when we are flirting or mentally entertaining other marriages, with fear, doubt, worry, anxiety or false beliefs.

9

A METAPHYSICAL UNDERSTANDING

Love is a state of oneness, a state of fulfillment.

We must never forget that Jesus was, and still is, a teacher.

He did not just leave some amusing stories for us to read. He left us instructions and examples.

That is why we need to understand the Bible for its metaphysical benefits.

In The Beginning:

God And Me

Genesis 1:26-28 *"And God said, let us make man in our image, after our likeness and let them have dominion over the fish of the sea, and over the fowl of the air, and over the cattle, and over every creeping thing that creepeth upon the Earth.*

So God created man in His own image, in the image of God created him; male and female created He them and He blessed them.

And God said unto them, be fruitful, and multiply, and replenish the Earth, and subdue it:

And have dominion over the fish of the sea, and over the fowl of the air, and over every living thing that moves upon the Earth."

Fish represent ideas of multiplication and fecundity, which is the capacity and quality for, or the power of producing in abundance; fertility.

In simple terms the power to produce fertile things in abundance.

Fowl of the air represents high lofty thoughts.

11

IN THE BEGINNING: GOD AND ME

Things of the Earth, the physical things necessary, are under my command.

You are made in His image likeness! The image likeness of God! What does that really mean?

Like God, I am the creator, the ruler of the universe, the almighty one with power and dominion.

I have the ability to think so I have the ability to obey and be fruitful, because of my fertility.

Also I am able to subdue anything and everything on Earth.

I have the ability to multiply because of my fertility and instructions from my Father to produce, to multiply.

I am the idea of my Father the one and only God.

I am His dream. He is expressing himself as me.

I am infinite; I have no boundaries or limits.

I am immeasurably and unaccountably large, and I am absolute good plus I am eternal.

So when I say "I am made in the image likeness of God", I am really saying something of tremendous importance. It is a plateau I can stand on as well as use for the betterment of my life, world and affairs.

All that God is I am, and all that God has is mine.

I am omnipresent, omniscient and omnipotent. (I am evenly present, all knowing, and all powerful.)

I am life, intelligence, love and power.

I am the temple, in which God lives.

I am that from which all love springs, and I am wisdom, power, strength and substance.

I am absolute wholeness and perfection.

Everything I have said is true about me and it is also true about you.

Well, if what you are saying is true Rev. Della, why am I catching it so hard? Why are things so bad? Why can't I get ahead no matter what I do?

It's because you have forgotten who you are. You have accepted the race consciousness, the human race consciousness with thoughts like:

"That's the way life is."..."You can't beat the boys downtown."..."They won't let us get through."..."It's all a no win situation."

You've given your power to money and greed has set in some form and to some extent.

IN THE BEGINNING: GOD AND ME

Greed begets hate and trickery and all things ungodly.

You have forgotten that when God made you He said, "This is good and very good."

This forgetfulness prompted disobedience and got us thrown out of bliss, which is what Eden means.

Every book from Genesis to Matthew, are allegories of roads back to bliss.

God in His love and by His grace, seeing our seeming inability to understand, sent His son Jesus to demonstrate the use of our powers, letting us see in the flesh, the power of our being made in the image likeness of God.

Jesus taught us that *"the Father and I and you are one."* Know that.

When asked why He had come He said, *"I have come that they might have life and that more abundantly."*

Follow me because I am the way, the truth and the light.

You are the light of the world and the salt of the earth.

He taught us we must thoroughly understand that God is spirit, in us.

He taught that we must understand our own personal relationship with God and His spirit within us. He taught us that there are tools we can use to help bring ourselves back to our senses.

The Holy Spirit is the action of God as He projects into our human consciousness.

He told us about faith and how to use it to bring from the invisible into the visible the things we wanted and the things we needed.

He described faith, as the rock, upon which, He would build His church.

What was His church?

What is your church?

They are one and the same.

Your church is an aggregation or groups of spiritual ideas in your individual consciousness.

You are your church, Jesus was His church, He thought right and therefore He taught right.

In the desert where Jesus lived and worked a solid rock was an important piece of real estate.

It was permanent and all around it was as the old hymn said, sinking sand.

The rock was permanent you could hang onto it, depend on its security and build on it to stand.

You could always expect it to support you and not just blow away as sand does.

What is the purpose of this lesson, Reverend Della?

Good question.

I submit to you that it is time to be the wise man or woman and build your life, starting this moment, on the rock of faith as Jesus taught us to do.

IN THE BEGINNING: GOD AND ME

I submit to you that it is possible to return to Eden through your faith. Start with faith in God.

Then, have faith in you.

Then have faith in the ideas that God will give you the improvements needed in your health, your mind, your body, and your being; for your relationships, your dreams, your desires, your general and specific fulfillments.

Refuse to continue to build on sand that keeps running through your fingers.

Faith is your eye to see the invisible. Faith holds your technique as well as your timing.

Faith is your peace of mind in your peace bank.

Faith is your joy in your joy bank. Faith is your measuring cup.

Faith is your fulfiller.

Faith helps you remember who you are.

You are all the things I started this lesson with and your faith in you and God will help you remember who and what you are and that you are made in the image likeness of God and all that entails.

We are the will of God, which is always perfection and all good.

We are an abundance of every good thing including joy, peace, wisdom, prosperity and eternal life.

The spirit of God within us is forever thinking thoughts of abundance, which is God's true nature.

Therefore because I am made in His image likeness, I must recognize and exercise my true nature which is abundance.

I am the image of omnipresent wealth, always present wealth.

I am the expression of the infinite riches of the universe; I am the individualization of lavish abundance because all that the Father is I am and all that the Father has is mine.

You really need to mentally accept what I am telling you. Your life depends on it.

> The Father and I are one, and all that the Father is, I am.

God Gave Us Dominion

At the risk of being redundant, as I said to you in chapter two, God personally gave us dominion . He told us to be fruitful, multiply and replenish the Earth and have dominion over the fish of the sea, fowl of the air, and everything on the Earth. We received authority from God to be just like Him.

Genesis 1:28. *"And God blessed them, and God said unto them, be fruitful and multiply and replenish the earth, and subdue it: and have dominion over the fish of the sea and over the fowl of the air and over every living thing that moveth upon the earth."*

In the 26th verse we received our authority from God to be just like Him, and He gave us dominion over everything that is on the face of this earth or in the sea.

The sea represents the mind of God.

Fish represents ideas of multiplication and fecundity, which is the quality or power of producing abundantly; which is productive or creative power.

Fowl represents high productive thoughts.

Because of our productive, creative powers, we have ideas of multiplication and the quality or power of

18

producing abundantly. We are simply using the authority that God gave us way back when He created us in the first place.

The question arises - What is really meant by the word dominion?

Dominion is control. It is the ability to exercise that control. It is sovereignty over a territory or sphere of influence or control. It is ownership rights.

God gave us this way back then when He first made us.

The 27th verse shows us He thought it was a good idea because He turned His words into action.

He blessed us and told us to be fruitful (produce abundantly). Not just babies, whatever we wanted to produce that is for our highest good.

He told us to subdue the earth and have dominion over every living thing that moves, upon the earth, even the creeping things.

Let me just add this: Every creeping thing that creepeth upon the earth is not some crawling thing. He didn't say every crawling thing. There are some 6-foot creeping things and some 5-foot 4-inch creeping things.

There are some family creeping things and some supposed friend creeping things, but you have dominion over them and God's authority to use your dominion.

God gave us mastery, which is having control over others, and other things, as owner and as possessor. Because of this mastery, whatever the situation or circumstance, if need be, we are able to subdue it. But we must be aware consciously of who and what we are in order to exercise our power. The acts of dominion and mastery produce sovereignty, which is supremacy of authority or rule.

The highest level of authority, God's authority, was given to us in the beginning.

Mastery is being a part of a mechanism that controls all other parts.

I don't know about you, but I am a part of that mechanism that controls all other parts. The Father and I are one.

When you read Gen. 1:29-31, you will find the other gifts He gave us then.

What is the point of this lesson, Rev. Del? I want to help you bring forth your ability to reason.

I want you to get the deeper understanding of your true position and the strength and sanctioning of your dominion and mastery given to you by the Father that loves you.

Your true abilities that you should be using for the purpose God gave them to you for the living of life and that more abundantly.

Stop being afraid; start being the power you really are. It has nothing to do with how you look, it's not what's on the box, it's what's in the box. It doesn't matter who your daddy was, where you came from or what you have done up to this point when you didn't truly understand your rightful position.

It has to do with accepting the truth of you and beginning right now to put your power to work.

GOD GAVE US DOMINION

You have power because dominion, mastery and sovereignty equal power. You have the power of God to be as effective in your life as Jesus was in His life.

Jesus told us greater things than He did we would do.

Recognize who you really are and begin to put your mastery and your dominion and your sovereignty to work for you.

Stop allowing the things of the world to take you over. Things have no power unless you give it to them.

You can do what you want to, but I refuse to give up such a tremendous gift from God in order to suffer and do without the abundance of peace, joy, understanding, prosperity, happiness, and the exciting adventure, of the exertion of my dominion, mastery and sovereignty in my daily living.

I accept the good that is rightly mine; designed by God, especially for me.

21

Made In His Image

Matthew 16:26 *"For what is a man profited, if he shall gain the whole world and lose his own soul? Or what shall a man give in exchange for his soul?"*

Genesis 1:26 *"And God said, let us make man in our image, after our likeness; and let them have dominion over the fish of the sea* (pregnant ideas) *and over the fowl of the air* (high quality ideas) *and the cattle* (the things physical)*, and over all the earth, and over every creeping thing, that creepeth upon the earth.*

1:27 *So, God created man in His own image, in the image of God created He him; male and female created He them."*

1:28 *And God blessed them, and God said unto them, be fruitful and multiply, and replenish the earth and subdue it; and have dominion over the fish of the sea and over the fowl of the air and over every living thing that moves upon the earth."*

I am, and so are you made in His image!

What does that really mean?

What is the image of God?

What is God? The Almighty One: the Creator, the ruler of the universe.

I am the image of the All Mighty one; I am the image of the creator of the universe, period!

I am infinite; I have no boundaries or limits.

I am immeasurably or unaccountably large.

I am eternal.

Why am I saying this? I want you to understand what you are made in the image of.

I am absolute good. I am omnipresent, omniscient, and omnipotent. I am in God wherever I am. God is in me wherever I am. The God in me has all the knowledge and all the power.

I am life, intelligence, love and power.

I am the temple in which God lives!

I am that from which all love springs.

I am wisdom, power, strength and substance.

I am absolute wholeness and perfection.

I am connected to God by my mind and my God-mind embraces all knowledge, wisdom and understanding, and is the source of every manifestation of true knowledge and intelligence.

The God principle I am is the unchangeable life, love, substance and intelligence of my being.

The Father and I are one. I am the will of God, which is always perfection and all good.

I am perfect health in mind and body.

I am an abundance of every good thing including joy, peace, wisdom and eternal life.

Now let's look at this.

Luke 9:25 *"For what is a man advantaged, if he gain the whole world, and lose himself, or be cast away."*

The soul is not Ray Charles or Aretha Franklin. It is not collard greens and ham hocks and corn bread either!

Soul is our consciousness; it is the man-accumulated ideas in back of our present expressions.

The original and also the true sense, of the soul of man is the expressed idea of man in God's mind.

We are spirit, soul, body. Spirit is the "I am," the individuality.

The body is soul expressing itself. Soul includes the conscious and subconscious minds.

Soul makes the body; the body is the outer expression of the soul.

Did you know bodily health is in exact correspondence to the health of the soul?

When there is soul development, there is unfoldment of divine ideals, in the soul, or consciousness, it brings the ideal into expression in the body.

So if you gain the world and lose your soul there is no advantage to you.

There is a great disadvantage. The disadvantage of blowing your connection to the source, to God.

You also have need to control the soul, do not lose it for health reasons, for ideas and ideals, for the sanctity of your mind, both your conscious, and your subconscious minds.

Our consciousness, our mind, are our connecting link to the Father which gives us all the knowledge, wisdom and understanding we need to survive and sustain and advance.

The spirit of God, within us, is forever thinking thoughts of abundance, which is God's true nature. Therefore because I am made in His image likeness I must recognize my true nature as abundance.

I am the image of omnipresent wealth, always present wealth!

I am the expression of the infinite riches of the universe.

I am the individualization of lavish abundance because all that the Father is I am and all that the Father has, is mine!

With this information embedded in my conscious mind and used by my heart (the subconscious mind).

My soul is the battery to energize me and show me the way to the success I am working toward.

You need to mentally accept what I am telling you.

I know it is a lot and for some of you it is hard to believe these things about yourself.

If you cannot mentally accept these things, you do not get your desired good no matter what else you do.

Those who cannot mentally accept greater abundance, never experience it.

Dare to release the past way of thinking, then mentally accept that this is the way that God planned it for you to have something better for yourself.

Your good has never rejected you but you are constantly rejecting your good.

God can only do for you what He can do through your mental attitudes.

Change your mind and change your life. Recognize how magnificent you are and mentally accept it.

Say this to yourself over and over:

> **I am magnificent.**

Put your power to work for you in the name of Christ Jesus.

Reject and stop believing the things, the people, and most of all the idea that you are not able nor equipped nor wise enough nor strong enough nor good enough nor "whatever" enough!

Whatever you have in your mind that makes you feel you're not "whatever" enough, reject it ferociously!

Change your mind right now and change your life.

Listen to the God inside of you that designed you to be the magnificence that He Himself is in every way, anytime and all the time.

Believe God first. Only believe God. Accept your wondrous power and use it to the glory of God.

With this knowledge you should walk around head high and strutting as the God you are, male and female!

Our souls are fed by thought; the true soul food is the word of God.

The word of God when properly used makes the soul immortal.

Don't loose your head, not for a minute. You need your head. Your brains are in it.

I feel the need to repeat some of the things I have already told you because it is important that you really get it. Repetition is a great way to lock in information you want to hold onto, and I absolutely want you to hold onto this information.

Our consciousness, our minds, are our connecting link to the Father which gives us all the knowledge, wisdom and understanding we need to survive and sustain and advance.

The spirit of God, within us, is forever thinking thoughts of abundance, which is God's true nature. Therefore because I am made in His image likeness I must recognize my true nature as abundance.

I am the image of omnipresent wealth, always present wealth!

I am the expression of the infinite riches of the universe. I am the individualization of lavish abundance because all that the Father is I am and all that the Father has is mine!

With this information embedded in my conscious mind and used by my heart (the subconscious mind), my soul is the battery to energize me and show me the way to the success I am working toward.

We need to mentally accept what I am telling you. I know it is a lot and for some of you it is hard to believe these things about yourself.

I repeat, if you cannot mentally accept these things you do not get your desired good no matter what else you do.

Those who cannot mentally accept greater abundance will never experience it.

Dare to release the past way of thinking. Then, mentally accept that this is the way that God planned it for you to have something better for yourself.

Your good has never rejected you, but you are constantly rejecting your good.

God can only do for you what He can do through your mental attitudes. Change your mind and change your life. Recognize how magnificent you are and mentally accept it. Repeat after me, "I am magnificent." Say it again!

Put your power to work for you in the name of Christ Jesus.

Reject and stop believing the things, the people, and most of all the idea that you are not able nor equipped nor wise enough nor strong enough nor good enough nor whatever enough!

Whatever you have in your mind that makes you feel you're not whatever enough, reject it ferociously!

Change your mind right now and change your life.

Listen to the God inside of you that designed you to be the magnificence, that He Himself is in every way, anytime and all the time.

Believe God first. Only believe God. Accept your wondrous power and use it to the glory of God.

With this knowledge you should walk around head high and strutting as the God you are, male and female!

I know what I have told you is so because Jesus told me so.

I manifest my real self, through this body right now.

I Am Responsible For My Life

Responsibility: the accountability for one's actions.

It is no longer possible or acceptable to pass the buck about your life.

I am responsible for my life and so are you responsible for yours.

If my life isn't working the way it should, I am responsible.

My mind is the instrument of my success.

I am the one with the greatest involvement in my life. I am the executive of this estate and I am responsible for my life.

I have thus far been speaking to you, but know this; I have to speak to myself also. I hope you will say these things to yourself and understand that it is true about you also.

God has given me power and dominion over all life, and my life, so I cannot blame my biological father; he was just part of my transportation from the other plane to this one. No matter if he was a good father or not.

I cannot blame my mother. She was the channel through which I made the trip from the other plane to this one.

I cannot blame the environment for I am able to choose my own environment. If I don't like where I am, I can move. It may take time and effort but I am equipped with all I need to move if moving is what is necessary.

I cannot blame the incidentals. My looks, my color, my education, my financial situation, if I am too fat I can become slimmer, if I am too slim I can gain weight. If I need education it is available.

The color story won't work for there are places in this world one can go to where it is not a problem at all. In fact, there are some countries that honor it.

I can pack up and go there or better still I can change my mind about it bothering me and stay right where I am and draw to me people who have no problem with it at all and appreciate me for it.

I am responsible for my life. I am responsible to God for my life.

Daniel Webster said it and we should all know it, as well as feel it deeply. "The most important thought that ever occupied my mind is that of my individual responsibility to God."

I am responsible to God for the thoughts I allow to fill my mind for He had one of His servants write me this message. "As a man/woman thinketh in his/her heart so is he/she." So, I am responsible to God for my thoughts for thoughts are things.

I am responsible for the things my life produces for He had His son to tell me.

I AM RESPONSIBLE FOR MY LIFE

Matthew 7:16-20 *"You shall know them by their fruits, every good tree brings forth good fruit, but a corrupt tree brings forth evil fruit. A good tree cannot bring forth evil fruit nor can a corrupt tree bring forth good fruit."*

He went on to tell us what would happen if we do not bring forth good fruit.

"Every tree that brings not forth good fruit shall be hewn down, and cast into the fire."

"Therefore you shall know them by their fruits."

I am responsible to God for my body. He told Paul to write me a letter about this body.

1 Corinthians 3:16-17 *"Know ye that ye are the temple of God and that the spirit of God dwelleth in you. If any man defile the temple of God him shall God destroy; for the temple of God is holy, and ye are that temple."*

"I am fearfully and wonderfully made."

He had Paul to tell me also that I should:

Romans 6:12-*14* *"Let not sin* (mistakes) *reign in your mortal body, that you should obey it in lust, neither yield ye your members as instruments of unrighteousness unto sin* (mistakes), *but yield yourselves unto God, as those that are alive from the dead, and your members as instruments of righteousness, unto God, for sin* (mistakes) *shall not have dominion over you; for you are not under the law; but under grace."*

So I am responsible for this body, this temple of God.

I AM RESPONSIBLE FOR MY LIFE

If I am not in my proper place I will have to work at it. If working for my success takes hours, I had better put in the required hours.

Whatever my success requires I had better hop to it for I am responsible for my success. Not conditions, or circumstances for, *"He that is in me is greater than he that is in the world."* All I have to do is remember the formula, *"All things, whatsoever I shall ask for in prayer, believing I shall receive."*

I am responsible for my life. God has delivered myself to my own care, therefore I have no one better designed to trust than me. There is no one more determined to preserve this person for me, than me. No one can nurture her nature of modesty, beauty, faithfulness, nobility, tranquility, creativity, but me; for I am the son of God in whom He is well pleased and who He sustains, because of my firm trust in His supreme powerfulness.

God's might directs me. God's power protects me. God's wisdom is mine to learn. God's eye is mine for discerning. God's ear is mine for hearing. God's work is mine for mind clearing.

I am not afraid, for I have a God I can trust to go with me and remain with me and be everywhere for my good. He lets me know that all will always be well.

I cannot allow myself to be anxious for the beginning of anxiety is the end of faith as the beginning of true faith is the end of anxiety.

He told me if I have faith the size of a mustard seed I can say to any mountain in my life "Be ye removed hence to yonder place"; and it shall be removed and nothing shall be impossible unto me.

He meant for me to know that because it is the equipment I need for I am responsible for my life.

You do whatever you want to with your temple, but I do not want my temple dirty or dark or negative or worn down with holes in the walls and disagreements between my executive branch and my working members.

He instructed me on that also, He had Jesus to tell me:

Luke 11:34-*36* *"The light of the body is the eye. Therefore when thine eye is single the whole body also is full of light; but when thine eye is evil the body is also full of darkness."*

"Take heed therefore that the light which is in thee be not darkness. If thy whole body therefore be full of light having no part dark, the whole shall be full of light, as when the bright shining of a candle doth give the light."

I want my light to shine, at least as bright as the lights on the strip in Vegas. I want the light inside and I want to encase that wonderful light with marvelous accompaniments.

I want the outside of my temple to look good also. I want the roof to look good. I want the auditorium of the temple to look good. I want the windows to shine with light. I want the floor to be clean and looking good. I want the walls to be decorated beautifully. I want my temple to be in an excellent, glorious, fantabulous condition because you see my God lives in here and my God deserves and must have only the exceptional good.

I am responsible to God for His habitat.

I AM RESPONSIBLE FOR MY LIFE

God designed me to succeed. I know that is true for He made me in His image/likeness.

So, I am responsible for my life, and the success of my life, my joy, my peace, my relationship with God.

Just as God has a commitment to me, I have a commitment to Him.

Thank God I have sense enough to really, really, really know for sure that I can never lose when God is what I choose.

In God I put my trust and I am not, and I will not be afraid of what anybody will say or what anything will try to do to me.

God is perfect harmony in my life and ALL of my experiences.

You Are Not Only Human, You Are Divine

Have you ever said, "I'm only human?" Well, you lied!

John 14:12 *"Verily, verily I say unto you, he that believeth in me* (the indwelling Christ), *the works that I do he shall do. Also greater works shall he do because I go unto the Father."* What does Jesus mean by this scripture? What is Jesus saying here really?

Because I have made this breakthrough, I have laid the foundation. I have opened up the way. I have shown you how to do it. And when there are different needs you will be able to do what is needed. Jesus was "on the road to overcoming" when He said, *"Follow me." "Come after me."* He was speaking as our Wayshower.

He knew (the Father intended it to be so) He was trailblazing.

"Follow Me" into greater awareness of the truth so you can see and demonstrate higher and higher overtones of the law.

Jesus was a man! Not an ordinary man; but a man. He was overcoming all along the way of His life just as we are.

Why? So we would be able to identify with Him.

Hebrews 4:15 *"For we do not have a high priest who cannot share our infirmities, but we have one who was tempted with everything we are, and yet without sin."*

Jesus had, as we do, the free will to choose. Jesus was without sin, not because He could not sin, but because He chose not to. He refused to sin. Sins are mistakes, and He knew following the words of His Father He did not have to make a mistake.

He worked on "self mastery," constantly! *"Not my will, but thine be done."*

Why do you think He had to say that?

He earned the right to be called master because of His victorious overcoming throughout His life.

That day on the Cross of Calvary, was commencement day for Jesus. He made "The Great Demonstration." He verified His teachings of the divinity of man!!! He proved dramatically that there is a depth in man, in you and I, far beyond the human depth.

Jesus was the great explorer of "inner space." He showed the "depth potential" of man.

Jesus proved conclusively the life of God is:

† Indestructible

† Changeless

† Eternal

Not just for Himself, alone, but for you and me too!

He proved we are able to rise above limited experiences and go forward through any dark hour to have a new beginning.

"He that is in me and you is greater than anything in the world."

When you see yourself in this larger context, you are free. You release your greatest potential. Then you are divine!!!

† No matter what you have been "conditioned to think" about yourself.

† No matter what you have done in or with your life.

† No matter how limited your life experiences seem to be.

† No matter who says whatever about it.

† No matter what is happening in your life at this moment that might give you the illusion it is otherwise...

You are divine!!! Made in the image likeness of your Father God who is divine.

You have come to know "want" in the forms of:

† Obstacles

† Handicaps

† Inharmonious experiences

† Illness

† Financial insecurity

They are appearances, not realities. I don't care, you are divine. Period! All you need to do is come out of the "far country" and back into your Father's house.

Wake up to your own divine potential. Wake up to the reality that you are divine. Know who you are and what you are.

Say it "I am divine" again louder, again sweeter, again with confidence because you accept the knowledge that it is the truth, "I am divine!"

I guess your question now is what is my divinity?

† That part of you that is ageless, deathless, whole and complete.

† That part of you that is perfect even when you seem to be imperfect.

† That part of you that "knows" when you are facing indecisiveness and fear.

† That part of you that can never be alone.

† That part of you that can never really be sick.

† That part of you that cannot be frustrated.

† That part of you, which is your indwelling Christ.

Wake up and let Christ shine through you, to you. Close your physical eyes that are fixed on appearances. Open your spiritual eyes see to the depth of Spirit.

You are immortal right now. The Christ of you, the divinity of you is immortal right here, right now.

That not only means you will live forever but it also means that in the midst of any experience, you can *"be still and know that I am God,"* and step into your limitless eternity.

You can get a new burst of confidence. New faith and new drive, more patience, a better understanding with new directions and a new flow of ideas, plus a new release of strength and whatsoever else you need.

Wake up and realize (see with your real eyes) that you are whole (holy) and you can go on to victory.

You will have a new consciousness, a new fearlessness, and a new confidence intuitively.

You will know that you are immortal and experience life more abundantly.

Life is for living. Life is not an experience of dying. Life is for growing and unfolding and expressing the "is-ness of God." Everything you will ever be you already are, right now.

Do not be mesmerized by appearances.

John 7:24 *"Judge not according to the appearance, but judge righteous judgment."*

Psalms 82:6,8 *"I have said, ye are Gods; and all of you are the children of the most high. Arise, o God, judge the earth; for thou shalt inherit all nations."*

John 10:34-35 *"Is it not written in your law, I said that ye are Gods; if He called them Gods, unto whom the word of God came, and the scripture cannot be broken."*

Romans 8:16-17 *"The spirit itself beareth witness with our spirit, that we are the children of God; and if children, then heirs; heirs of God, and joint-heirs with Christ;"*

It is written in the law, and it is declared to be so, by "Christ Jesus," therefore, it cannot be changed.

All that is left is for us to accept this truth and rise up to it.

I am not just human, I am divine!!! You are not just human you are divine!!! We are not just human we are divine!!! And so it is and Amen.

Speak these words of truth into your consciousness.

I am in tune with God and I can do whatsoever needs to be done whenever, I need to do it.

I am success oriented so I succeed. I am an overcomer so I continually overcome.

I can be and do whatsoever I want, that is for my highest good, because the Christ in me sees things rightly and is all the power, all the knowledge, all the energy and ability and capability I need.

The kingdom of Heaven is in me now; it is not somewhere to go to. It is something I am able to be.

I am without as I am within - Christ like.

It is my Father's good pleasure to give me the kingdom. I am in Heaven when I am in my upper consciousness expanding in my Christ consciousness.

Christ in me is my hope of glory.

I have made the great discovery for myself.

Is Your Attitude
Your Ally Or Your Enemy?

Attitude: Manner, disposition, feeling, position, tendency, orientation of the mind regarding a person or situation.

Your attitude does make a difference.

What kind of difference is your attitude making? Is it an ally or an enemy?

Have you ever said, "I just don't like his attitude"?

And if you will, remember that dislike kept you from doing anything for, with or about that person.

And you had the feeling you had to do something to get away from that person as quickly as possible? Do you remember that?

A nasty attitude is the quickest way to be alone.

Nobody needs to be bothered with an attitude that is unpleasant, angry, hostile, confused, uncaring, belligerent, hateful, evil, selfish, dull or non-productive.

IS YOUR ATTITUDE YOUR ALLY
OR YOUR ENEMY?

In your home, a bad attitude can keep constant confusion alive and active, and won't allow compromise or adjustments.

In the work place, a bad attitude can stop advancement and good working relationships.

In human relationships, a bad attitude is a sure way of losing friends. Do you make talking to you a problem because of your attitude?

Because you are so paranoid that you misinterpret or misunderstand and turn the other person to explanation instead of communication? Do you expect troubles and problems and draw them to you because of your attitude, which repels the people you say your life needs, and attracts the ones you say you don't want because you have an incompatible attitude?

Well, you get what you expect.

Do you believe you have to watch everybody because nobody can be trusted?

Do you believe, whatever it is, if you want it done right, you have to do it yourself (because other people are so dumb or inept they will surely mess it up)?

So, you have to do everything yourself, then you complain, about how tired you are, because you have to do everything yourself?

Do you make everyone responsible for what has happened to you before you met them?

And want them to dance to the music of your bad experiences and then get disappointed when they refuse and then splice each new experience into the old tape?

44

IS YOUR ATTITUDE YOUR ALLY
OR YOUR ENEMY?

Attitudes do make a difference!

A person with a winning attitude is a winner. The person with a losing attitude is a loser. When you have a winning attitude your body shows it by your posture.

The body language of a loser is very different from that of a winner.

The actions and emotions of a winner are vastly different from those of a loser.

A loser is paranoid, always emotionally upset, the world is against him. Nothing ever works out for him but he will not understand that it is up to him. In his mind it is always somebody else's fault.

A winner believes everybody wants him to win. He's happy about it. He believes in his ideas. He gets behind them and works with an anticipation of success because he never believes he's going to fail.

And if things do go off on him, he has the courage to rise and try again because in his mind he is a winner, he has a winner's attitude and he/she feels it is just a matter of time before the great victory will be his because if this idea doesn't come into fruition he's got plenty more where that one came from.

Right attitudes make you effective in dealing with people. Right attitudes enable you to develop as a leader. Right attitudes win for you in every situation.

Philippians 2:5-6 *"Let this mind be in you that was in Christ Jesus; who being in the form of God thought it not robbery to be equal with God."*

Jesus knew who and what He was. He knew what He could do. His attitude was that He and the Father were one and He would succeed in whatever the Father sent Him to do.

We need to have in us the mind (the attitude) that was in Christ Jesus. We need to grow the attitude of, "I am activated by the power of my Father inside me."

Our attitudes should be as Jesus' *"Of myself I can do nothing. It is the Father inside me that does the works, and all things are possible, through this power of, my Father, inside me."*

Grow the attitude of "I am important because I am the temple of God."

"I am important because God needs me to do His will and His work."

To activate others you must be activated yourself.

You must be enthusiastic.

You must think you and your ideas are important, because you and your ideas are both of God.

You must enjoy serving if you want to be served.

You must know who your source is so that you don't have to lean and depend on people or conditions for your supply.

God is your source. Not people. Not your job. Not your mate. Not your children. God and God alone.

You need to know about your spiritual inheritance. You need a believing attitude.

You need to start each day and each project knowing that God is helping you and "If God is for you, and He is, who can stand against you?"

If you want to receive you must have a giving attitude.

Giving is the first step to receiving.

Give to God, give to you, and give to others.

This is the way you prepare for wealth. Speak words of receiving, not of lack and limitation.

If your attitude is that there is not enough, there will not be enough for you. Because whatever you say it is, in your life, it is in your life. So if you say there is not enough, there will not be enough for you.

You must daily declare "God is supplying and I am receiving all that I need for life and that more abundantly."

Declare daily, *"God is my sufficiency in all things."* Assume that attitude! Walk like it, talk like it, think like it and react like it.

Attitudes make little people feel big and make big people feel even bigger.

Don't criticize and condemn.

Have the attitude that the other person is a child of God just like you and has the inherited right to succeed just as you do.

Do all you can to make them feel that way. Do all you can to help them on their way. For your sake not theirs because the law is that as you sow, so shall you reap.

IS YOUR ATTITUDE YOUR ALLY
OR YOUR ENEMY?

By helping him or her you are helping yourself.

Have the attitude of appreciation. Stop taking people and things for granted.

Nobody has to give you a burnt match. I don't have to do anything for you. Your attitude makes me want to do something for you. People thrive on compliments, not complaints.

Do you limit yourself to a small group that you love?

Jesus said if you only love your friends and family, so what? You have to learn to love all God's children.

Don't hog the glory.

To God be the glory in the first place.

So do what has to be done to the glory of God.

When you do it for the doing, not for the credit, the accolades will flow freely to you.

Get some correct information before you start judging people and things.

You usually don't like something because you don't know anything about it.

Jesus says, *"Judge not so you won't be judged but if you must judge, judge not by appearances, judge the righteous judgment,"* If you have to judge at all.

If you think about it you will be able to act about it with the right attitude, which most often is to give yourself the advice to mind your own business.

48

IS YOUR ATTITUDE YOUR ALLY
OR YOUR ENEMY?

You claim to be a Christian. A Christian is a follower of Christ - people who believe and act as Christ believes and acts.

How can you be Christ-like and not lift Christ up in your life?

The Gospel is good news not complaints and despair.

Smile at people, thank them, encourage them, compliment them, really listen to them when they speak, be helpful, make people feel important.

Why?

Because, you would rather people smile at you, than frown at you about the things you do. Because you too want to be thanked and appreciated for what you do.

Because you need encouragement and compliments. Because you want to be really listened to.

Help because you need to help make people feel important, because you need to feel important from some "God with skin on it" sometimes.

Feeling important is man's strongest, most compelling, non-biological hunger.

People do more for you when you make them feel important.

Praise is power.

Give people more than they expect, this is the instruction Jesus gave us.

Matthew 5:40-42, 48 *"And if any man will sue thee at the law and take away your coat, let him*
49

have the cloak also. And whosoever shall compel thee to go a mile, go with him twain (two miles), *give to him that asks you, and from him that would borrow of you turn not away, be ye therefore perfect, even as your Father which is in Heaven* (inside you) *is perfect."*

You cannot obey this if you live in an attitude of lack and limitation. You can only do this if you live in an attitude of abundance knowing that there is more than enough to share and spare.

You need a receiving attitude. Is your mind open to receive? Or is your mind closed up and you're receiving channels plugged up with fear, doubt and confusion, anger, anxiety, hate and the likes?

Receive means accept whatever you believe you must receive.

If you believe the world is against you, you must receive the world is against you. If you believe it's too good to be true you must receive it's too good to be true.

Nothing is too good to be true, only good is true.

Stop fighting your good and receive it.

You never know who God is sending it by, so stop turning people off and away. They might be the bearers of your good.

There is a scripture that says be careful who you turn away from your door. It might be an angel.

Have the attitude of a child of the king. "It is my Father's good pleasure to give me the kingdom."

Believe it and receive it.

IS YOUR ATTITUDE YOUR ALLY
OR YOUR ENEMY?

You need a new attitude. An attitude of giving, knowing that your brothers and sisters are God's children too.

An attitude of being God activated.

An attitude of importance, an attitude of appreciation, an attitude of praise, the attitude, and mind that was in Christ Jesus.

The attitude that right now you are receiving all the wealth the universe has for you.

Say this to yourself:

> Right now, I am receiving all the wealth the universe has for me, for I have in me the mind and attitude that was in Christ Jesus: who, being in the form of God thought it not robbery to be equal with God.
>
> I've got a new attitude!

Do unto others as you would have them do unto you, but as a Christ follower you do it first.

Be Of These Attitudes

Jesus knew that our opinions are formed and are the basis for our attitudes, so He in His teachings, told us how to work with our attitudes.

Therefore our opinions, which are our beliefs, can be held with confidence, so that our attitudes, can be substantiated, by positive knowledge, which is proven by the working of our faith.

Jesus gave us an evaluation or judgment based on special knowledge given to Him by an expert, our Father God.

Our attitudes are our manner of handling things. Attitudes create our dispositions, and our feelings, which decide our positions, which produce our tendencies; and our inclinations to think, act, or behave in a certain way which controls the orientation of the mind regarding people or situations.

Our disposition is our customary manner of emotional response better known as our temperament; which is an inclination especially when it is habitual.

BE OF THESE ATTITUDES

Jesus knew that your attitude can, and will project you forward or hold you back and keep you back. Attitudes make a difference!

Your attitude about troubles and problems draw them to you.

Your attitude repels the people you say your life needs and attracts the ones you say you don't want, because your attitudes are more compatible with the "don't want" group.

With the Sermon on the Mount, Jesus is telling us the attitudes that will bring us peace of mind, mastery of our lives, and the prosperity in every way that He came to teach us to own.

Matthew 5:3 *"Blessed are the poor in spirit for theirs is the kingdom of Heaven."* Poor in the spirit of selfishness, poor in the spirit of haughtiness, phoniness, poor in the spirit of personal consciousness, and rich in the spirit of Christ. To be willing to empty yourself of all desire to exercise personal will.

Why?

Because when you get yourself out of the way and let the Christ inside of you take control, willingly, you enter into the kingdom of Heaven inside you.

Matthew 5:4 *"Blessed are they that mourn for they shall be comforted."*

Mourn: to express or feel grief.

There are people and things dying in our lives daily. Dreams, ideas, respect for people, disillusions, things that make us mourn. When we mourn, if at no other time, we eventually turn to God and that is where we find real comfort, a comfort that nothing or no one

53

else can give us.

So don't feel bad about feeling so bad, IF you let it turn you to the Father. Some people can't seem to turn to Him any other way.

In this respect, trouble can be a blessing in disguise, because it causes you to turn to God for guidance and supply.

Blessed are they that experience sorrow with a resolve to learn from it. Sorrow expands us as it shakes us up and causes us to grow. The experience of the presence of God is the end of all mourning.

Matthew 5:5 *"Blessed are the meek, for they shall inherit the earth."*

Meekness is a mental attitude. Meekness is the secret to success in prayer.

To conform to the will of God could only mean a finer and better life.

To be meek is not to be weak. In fact it takes great strength to be meek.

The first step to meekness is the ability to listen and obey. To be teachable, willing to learn and practice positive, prosperous thinking.

When you are meek, you are highly trained to react to all negative stimuli with love instead of the eye for an eye attitude.

The meek are not weak. When they dare to forgive and release the hurts of the past, they open the way to receive greater good in the present.

To be meek is to be quietly and firmly positive yet

flexible, adaptable, and able to forget, dismiss and release thoughts of past hurt, loss, failure or disappointment.

With the right attitudes, you inherit the Earth and the abundance of your outer world will come forth showing happy results.

To inherit the Earth means to claim the dominion that is your divine heritage over the limiting experiences of life such as ill health, insufficient supply, indebtedness, inharmony, and loneliness.

Matthew 5:6 *"Blessed are they that do hunger and thirst after righteousness: for they shall be filled."*

Hunger and thirst: intense longings.

Those who hunger and thirst after the right use of God ideas shall find their lives filled with abundant blessings.

Those who hunger and thirst after God ideas which are prosperous ideas, find their lives filled with the blessing of health, wealth and happiness.

Righteousness: right thoughts followed by right actions.

To think and act in a just, upright, and harmonious manner.

Righteousness is not merely right conduct, but right thinking on all subjects in every department of your life.

A wholehearted search for truth and righteousness shall be crowned with success.

Matthew 5:7 *"Blessed are the merciful, for they shall obtain mercy."*

You are blessed if you hold merciful attitudes toward others.

When you do, they too shall be prospered and lovingly blessed.

Unmerciful attitudes are criticism, condemnation, hate, revenge, any falseness, lying, cheating, acts prompted by greed.

These attitudes cause more indebtedness and financial worry than any other state of mind.

When someone's weakness comes to your attention, they are unconsciously calling for your blessing, and what goes around comes around. Which is the law of sowing and reaping.

I am blessed by being merciful to, and thinking mercifully about you. For when I need it, I shall find mercy.

The true thought about your brothers and sisters is that there is a piece of God in us all.

Whatever the situation when true thoughts are included they bless both your sisters and brothers and you spiritually.

Matthew 5:9 *"Blessed are the peacemakers for they shall be called the children of God."*

When you make or even keep the peace, you are like your Father or your Brother Jesus.

You have that quality in you that will bring about a peacefulness just by your entrance into a room when you bring forth the Christ inside you.

I am not talking about meddling. I am talking

about being.

Being filled with the spirit of God and letting it flow through you into the situation or circumstance.

Matthew 5:10 *"Blessed are they which are persecuted for righteousness' sake; for theirs is the kingdom of heaven"* (in which they can rest and be rejuvenated and prepare for the return to strength and faith).

Matthew 5:11 *"Blessed are you, when men shall revile you, and persecute you and shall say all manner of evil against you falsely, for My sake."*

Both the Father and Jesus know how just plain mean and hateful people can be especially if you are trying to live the life of Christ.

They both know how people will attack you and your faith and your right to serve God the way you see to be right for you if it disagrees with what they think.

If you will think about this lesson and reason it out to yourself, you will vividly see what Jesus is teaching us and why.

The price for liberty is eternal vigilance.

If you really want to demonstrate health, happiness and true prosperity, to demonstrate these things as soon as you possibly can, which I must add is the duty of every truth student and metaphysician, you need to set aside a definite time every day for prayer and meditation, and for checking up on your own daily conduct and demonstrations.

This is how the Father is glorified in the Son.

People can be a pain in the lower posterior, but I

can live above that. You can too! It puts us in the class of the greatest, knowing they did it to the prophets and to Jesus, know that you can do as they did, go into the kingdom of God inside you and rest and reconnoiter and return to the battlefield renewed.

Jesus is teaching us that we need to conduct the affairs of our lives, minds, souls and beings in business-like manner.

Too many people fail to realize that the business of spiritual growth calls for order, method, and intelligent organization. Just as much, I believe even more, as any commercial business or engineering enterprise or other important activity; if it is to be a success.

Jesus is giving us our spiritual platform. That is the giving attitude He possesses. To be like Him, we must have the attitude of giving.

The plain fact is that it is the law of life that, as we think and speak and act toward others, so will others think and speak and act toward us.

Whatever we give out will inevitably be given back to us.

This in no way means that the same people whom we treat well or ill will be the actual people to return the action. In fact, that is very, very rarely the case.

What does happen is that some other person at some other time and place, often far away and sometimes long afterwards, who know absolutely nothing of your previous action, will nevertheless repay you. Grain for grain, pressed down, shaken together and running over.

Every unkind word,

every time you cheat,

every time you deceive,

every time you lie,

every time you neglect a duty,

evade a responsibility,

you are going to get it brought back to you.

The law of retribution is a cosmic law, it is as impersonal and unchanging as the law of gravity; neither considering persons nor respecting institutions; without rancor but without pity; therefore it behooves us to think twice or more times before we treat others unjustly.

But it is a poor law that doesn't work both ways and so it is equally true that for every good deed that you do and every kind word you speak, you will in the same way at some time or other get back the equivalent.

Understanding this should help you to be of the attitudes Jesus taught us.

Repeat the statements on the next two pages aloud to yourself:

With this information, if I will adopt it sincerely into my conscious awareness, will lead me to the attitude and understanding that my God given attitude is I am power for success.

Because of my intense longings for God, I hunger and thirst for Him.

I am power in a positive way.

Because my attitude is, that my spirit is poor in the spirit of selfishness and my personal consciousness is rich in the spirit of Christ.

Because of my attitudes, I am health, I am strength, I am peace because I am a "peace maker," and the peace in me gives peace to others.

I am happiness; I am prosperity because the kingdom of Heaven is mine.

I am strong, well and vital. I am happy and free. I am eternally youthful and I am poised because of my attitudes.

I do not depend upon persons or conditions for my prosperity. God is the source of my supply, and God provides His own amazing channels of supply for me right now!

My prosperity now comes to me from expected and unexpected channels in expected and unexpected ways, from all points of the universe, rich supply comes to me.

This is my attitude and I will not try in any other way to gain the world for I have given my soul to God and I won't take it back so I can lose it!

Equal To Jesus

Philippians 2:5-6 *"Let this mind be in you which was also in Christ Jesus; who being in the form of God, thought it not robbery to be equal with God."*

Jesus said we should be equal to Him. It is a challenge, it is a challenge I ask you to undertake starting now.

To be equal to Jesus you have to know something about Jesus.

Jesus is our Wayshower, our savior because He discovered the indwelling Christ the real savior. He showed us how to get in touch with that indwelling Christ.

The Bible says in **Luke 2:52**, *"Jesus increased in wisdom and stature and in favor with God and man."*

So Jesus had to grow wiser and stand taller to entrench Himself, deeper in favor with God, which gave Him power to gain favor with man, with us.

Jesus grew and we must grow.

Becoming equal is a growing process.

If you decide to take this assignment, don't expect it to be easy, just victorious. You have to do as Jesus told His father and mother.

Luke 2:49 *"I am in my Father's house taking care of my Father's business."* He left mother, father and everybody else if they didn't want to understand and follow God. Know this just as Mary and Joseph did not understand and were afraid and angry with Jesus, trying to stop Him, so will those around you try to stop you.

You have to do as Jesus did, release them and let them stand on their own two spiritual feet.

Alright Rev. Della, what is required to be equal with Jesus? What do I do? What you must do is answer these questions within yourself and for yourself:

† Do you believe that Jesus Christ is your Wayshower, your brother?

† Do you believe the indwelling power that is Christ is in you?

† Are you willing to travel from the human consciousness to spiritual consciousness?

† Are you willing to travel through your mixed state of consciousness? Because you cannot use your power, in a mixed state, of consciousness.

Once you have settled these issues within yourself, the Christ consciousness will be opened to you as you praise and give thanks to God. Then you can go to the city of David, Jerusalem, which is the habitat of peace. There is a nerve center just at the back of your heart; from this nerve center, the love center, spirit sends its radiance through the entire body.

You have to leave Nazareth, which is just a

63

branch, an offshoot of the true vine, God, and journey to a place on the banks of the River Jordan, where John the Baptist is preaching to be baptized. The water of baptism symbolizes a cleaning process. The getting rid of the limited thoughts that are encumbering and darkening your understanding. The water of baptism symbolizes a cleansing process, the letting go of error. It is the first step to the realization of truth. We cannot get into the new consciousness until we get rid of the old.

Nazareth was a despised place (the things of the spirit of God are considered foolish by the natural man). Nazareth was considered a community of common place people, if not disreputable people.

It is asked once, "Can anything good come out of Nazareth?" Nevertheless, in this commonplace village, Jesus was reared: and in the seemingly mediocre mind, the Christ truth is received and expressed. Nazareth typifies the commonplace mind of man, but it is a place of development through which the Christ came into expression.

So what does that mean?

No matter where you are, even in a place as disrespected as Nazareth, you too can develop the Christ in you.

You have to cross over Jordan which is in all of us a stream of thought constantly flowing through the subconscious mind. Good thoughts, bad and indifferent, which is typified in scripture as the River Jordan.

It is the life flow to thought through you from head to toe.

In our ignorance, in our unredeemed state, the Jordan is muddy with sense concepts and turbulent with material thoughts.

This stream of thought is your adversary. And when these reverse thoughts are removed, it then expresses itself as the life current.

The adverse thoughts in your mind have spread themselves over the underlying God consciousness, and have dammed up the free flow of divine energies in you, cutting off your divine expression.

This adverse consciousness will disturb you as long as you believe in the presence or power of evil. The sooner we students of truth come to the conclusion that the subconscious realm of mind, the part of the mind which we are most concerned about bringing into the light, is under the control of our God mind, the quicker we will set into activity, in the body, the power of the inherent spirit and the sooner we will bear the fruits of God in our flesh.

Substance (God) awaits the demands of the "I am Man," the Christ in you and then it (God) shapes itself according to your thoughts and works upon your demands.

So what do we have to do, Rev. Della? Change the way you use your thoughts. Change your mind to have in you the mind that was in the mind of Christ Jesus.

Be transformed by the renewing of your mind!

That's why I tell people the same thing all the time. Change your mind, change your life.

I teach that all the time because there is no other way.

Neither God, nor Jesus, nor situation, nor conditions can change for you if you continue to think the same thoughts; because thoughts are things and when you keep thinking the same thoughts, you must keep producing the same things.

If you want a new crop of experiences, if you want peace instead of problems, if you want prosperity instead of poverty, change your mind and change your life, world and affairs.

It isn't easy. Jesus never said it would be easy. It wasn't easy for Jesus but He stuck with it until it was completed.

What you call the devil represents a mass of negative thoughts that have been built up in your consciousness. Another name for the devil is sense consciousness; all the thoughts that are in you that are opposed to God.

Fear thoughts, sick thoughts, jealous thoughts, gossip thoughts, mean thoughts, lying thoughts, hate-filled thoughts, conniving thoughts, all belong to the state of mind called the devil.

Jesus met the same temptations that you and I are meeting today.

He overcame them, He met anger with forgiveness, and He met resentment with love.

Say this aloud to yourself, thinking about what you are saying:

Let this mind be in me which was also in Christ Jesus, who being in the form of God, thought it not robbery to be equal with God.

And I, as Jesus, being in the form, the image likeness of God, think it not robbery to be equal with Jesus who is equal to God.

I ask you in all sincerity and compassion help me Lord to prove this in my life.

This is new thinking for me, this is the new truth I want to replace all my negative thinking with. I ask your strength to help me strengthen my power.

I accept that it is already done because I know you always hear me when I pray and you answer in love and mercy. Thanks God for my new beginning.

If You Go To The Mountain, You Can Walk The Water

We are on a never-ending journey to be equal with Jesus. There are some things we need in our "carry-on" luggage. We need a deep understanding so we need to carry it close where it is readily available.

I want to tell you about two things we need right now: water and the mountain.

What kind of water are we to deal with? What aspects are represented by water?

There are many different aspects represented by water.

† Cleansing

† Mental potentiality

† Life

† Energy

† Weakness

† Negativeness

IF YOU GO TO THE MOUNTAIN,
YOU CAN WALK THE WATER

When we allow ourselves to become negative to the goodness of God, we find ourselves uncertain and unstable in our minds, which:

† Will make your body ill

† Fill you with discouragement and disappointment

† Will make you want to give up to the weakness of the undertow

That is why we must constantly remind ourselves that God is good all the time.

"My grace is sufficient for thee; for my strength is made perfect in weakness."

This is Jesus speaking to Paul. He was really saying to Paul, you have nothing to worry about because you have remembered that I am your strength.

Listen to Paul speaking to the Corinthians

2 Corinthians12:9-10 *"Most gladly therefore will I rather glory in my infirmities, that the power of Christ may rest upon me. Therefore I take pleasure in infirmities, in reproaches, in necessities, in persecution, in distresses for Christ's sake; (for the faith I have in Jesus Christ) for when I am weak, then I am strong."*

Understand Paul was not a masochist. He was not enjoying the pain and infirmities and reproaches and all the rest of it any more than we do.

You can just rejoice and be glad because, you know, there is nothing to worry about; because I will provide what you need to handle it, whatever it is, for I am your sufficiency. If we can accept this, it will make us buoyant enough to walk the water if we have to.

Matthew 14:23-31 talking about Jesus. *"And when He had sent the multitudes away, He went up into the mountain apart to pray."*

Mountain metaphysically means exaltation, a higher place of consciousness, a state of spiritual realization. And when evening had come, He was there alone.

But the ship was now in the midst of the sea, tossed with waves; for the winds were contrary.

And in the fourth watch of the night, Jesus went unto them walking on the sea.

When the disciples saw Him walking on the sea, they were troubled saying, "It is a spirit," and they cried out of fear.

But straight way Jesus spoke unto them, saying, "Be of good cheer; it is I; be not afraid."

And Peter answered Him and said, "Lord, if it is you, bid me come unto thee on the water."

And Jesus said, "Come," and when Peter was come down out of the ship, he walked on the water to go to Jesus. But when he saw the wind was boisterous, he was afraid; and beginning to sink, he cried, saying, "Lord, save me."

Immediately, Jesus stretched forth His hand, and caught him, and said unto him, "O thou of little faith, wherefore didst thou doubt?"

Peter didn't know how to walk by faith and not by

sight.

Peter was in the learning stages at that time. Peter is a perfect example of the faith, of some of the people of today.

Their faith is wavering and they deny it when they should embrace it closest to themselves.

When faith works through the intellect, it is subject to all the winds and waves of sense thought, sense consciousness.

Because with your conscious mind, you are always trying to make it logic when it is belief.

But when it works through life and God substance, Jesus said, *"The gates of Hell shall not prevail against it."*

Peter wavered in his faith because he was not established in love.

Faith is so important that Jesus said, *"It is the rock upon which I build my church."*

Jesus did not mean on Peter the man! He meant on "petros" which is the rock.

You must keep your eye on Peter at all times, at all costs.

Make him take care of business every minute.

Teach him to affirm truth all the time, over and over and over at least three times.

You have to teach Peter to concentrate.

He is inquisitive, impulsive and dictatorial, when

not firmly directed.

When Peter makes you question your dominion and tries to dictate the movements of your other powers, put him in his place as Jesus did. *"What matter that to thee? You follow me."*

When you become more aware of the presence of the living God substance inside of you, the more you activate your power. When the storms come and the waves and winds are contrary, if you will go to the mountain, you can walk the water, storms, winds, whatever, whenever you have to.

All you have to do is keep your eye and your mind on the Christ inside you and never look at the contrary winds and waves.

When you don't seem to know which way to go, your faith is your forward motion power. It assures your ability to walk the water if you have to.

If you need to change the way things are going in your life, faith is the transforming and transferring power to make you buoyant enough to walk the water when you have to.

To walk the water of troubled thoughts without sinking requires the established faith of Jesus in the saving power of the spirit.

The sea represents God and mental potentiality.

The human race has formed a sea of thought, and to walk over it safely requires that we have faith in ourselves as well as God.

We need to have an understanding of God, an understanding of the law of mastery given to us and

72

an understanding of ourselves. In order to walk on the waves of troubled thoughts caused by emotions without sinking, you must become established in the faith of spirit through the Christ inside of you.

You may find you have the need to cry out, "O Lord, save me." Rest assured if you do, Jesus will immediately stretch out His hand and catch you, saving you from drowning.

He will not let you sink!

He will speak about your faith as He holds you up until you know that all of God's good is for you, is in you, waiting for the call by your faith to bring it into manifestation.

Remember whenever you need to, you can send the multitude away and go up into the mountain apart and pray. You can always go into a high place, a higher level of consciousness, a state of spiritual realization and be apart, alone with the Christ inside of you and prepare yourself to walk the water whenever you have to.

The reason Jesus could feed 5,000, walk the water, raise the dead, get money from the fishes mouth, heal the sick, go through the cross and the tomb to the resurrection, was because in His "carry on" luggage He had faith in God. In all these occasions and according to His faith, it was done unto Him and according to your faith; it will be done unto you.

If you go to the mountain, you can walk the water any time you have to.

When the waters of my life are raging, I go to the mountain, and I can walk the raging waters.

Excusitis

Many of you are dealing with a terrible disease. It is not so much a physical disease as it is a hindering disease, paralyzing disease.

This disease is the answer to the questions many of you ask often. "I'm doing the best I can. Why can't I seem to get ahead?"

God has no respect of person. We are all made in His image likeness... not like the image and likeness. We are the image likeness... we are just like God. That is how we are designed.

So God knowing He designed you to be perfect... knows whatever it is you can handle it and if not, you will turn to Him for whatever assistance you need, for He is constantly available, evenly present and accessible to you.

Therefore, if you don't say anything to Him, He is saying, "He/she will work it out in time. She/he's got all the needed equipment."

You have heard Him say so to you when you say, "I can't do this!" You hear something inside you say, "Yes you can. You can do this."

EXCUSITIS

If you have never heard it, turn up your hearing aid because the Christ inside you is talking to you all the time.

Your mama used to tell you it was your conscience. What it really is, is God speaking to you through the Christ inside you. It's always clear even though sometimes, most times, you deny it. Then later we hear you say, "If I had followed my first mind." (your God mind)

Making money, having joy, having peace of mind; having the love you want and the love you need... sometimes are two different things. You don't know about that, huh?

You can do all of that by healing yourself of the disease I spoke to you about earlier.

What disease, Rev. Della?

Excusitis.

I used to have it and I had it bad but I am standing before you now cured, healed.

Excusitis is a fatal disease.

It will stand firmly between you and your good. Successful people are less inclined to make excuses.

Excuses are things to hide behind and you can always find something to hide behind.

Excuse is seeking indulgence. Excuse is to request exemption from an obligation or a duty.

Excuse is a plea or explanation offered to elicit pardon.

EXCUSITIS

Excuses are for those that fall short of certain standards or expectations.

"My mama was mean to me, my father didn't treat me right, my teacher in school called me one of those names... my boss is a drag... my wife isn't too wonderful no more... my husband's acting strange... and those kids are driving me mad... I don't have enough time... I don't have enough education... I am black... I am Jewish... I have to do everything and nobody appreciates what I do anyway!"

Excusitis makes one an excellent liar. You have to be to remember all the lies you have to keep up with.

Three months ago, you made an excuse using the dog. You meet the same people and they ask, "How is your dog?"

"The dog? Oh, oh, yeah the dog... well the dog is... well you know dog... er, ah..." Another lie.

You know you do that and it makes you stay in a continuous lying pattern.

It happens because you say you don't want to offend.

How could you offend me more than by lying to me?

Just say, "No thank you" and when they ask why, say "Because I don't want to." But you can't do that. You'd rather kill off your husband.

"No."

"Why not?"

EXCUSITIS

"Well, my husband is so sick..."

And you almost put your husband in the grave. Or you say:

"He gets such an attitude..."

You just gave him a bad character reference.

Men do this also.

I refuse to kill or embarrass or lie about on my husband Franklin.

If that stops us from being friends because I don't want to have dinner or whatever, we were never friends in the first place. You were just looking for a place to jump ship!

I am not going to swear to you so you will believe what I say.

Matthew 5:34-37 *"Swear not at all; neither by heaven for it is God's throne, nor by the Earth for it is His footstool, neither by Jerusalem for it is the city of the great king. Neither shalt thou swear by thy head, because you cannot make one hair white or black. But let your communication be, yea, yea; nay, nay; for whatsoever is more than this comes of evil."*

When I hear someone say, "The Lord is my secret judge," I say, "Let me out of here, cause here comes a lie."

"I swear on my mother's grave."

Redd Foxx had a wonderful way to swear. "If I'm lying, let God strike me dead right here." Then he'd step to another place.

EXCUSITIS

There are various degrees of excusitis. There are five I'd like to mention here.

† The age thing. "I'm over the big 50."

† "My health ain't what it used to be. My back... my knee... my whatever is in such bad shape."

† "My money is so short I can't help myself. I sure can't help anybody else."

† "This can't work. Nothing ever works for me."

† When ladies have feminine days, they give birth to those headachy night excuses.

That is the time you need love reinforced instead of the excuse "my head hurts." Why not just ask for what you really want and need?

She says: "I just need you to hold me right now... could you rub me a little bit, Daddy?"

It goes the other way also. He says: "Daddy's a bit tired tonight. Could you just rub Daddy's back for him?"

The excuses tell you that you have to trick each other into providing what you need.

Excuses equal failure. You've heard this, I know. "When the iron is hot, strike it." Excuses make you procrastinate and by the time you get ready to strike the iron, it is cold and the opportunity has moved on to somebody else.

Excuses are deceptive. They will keep you from giving God the credit and the glory.

I've had people come to me for consultation and

they have said to me, "I've been praying to God about this for two years or a year or for some length of time and I haven't gotten an answer yet."

I pray with them and we make a connection with God. The next time they return, they say, "You're not gonna believe this. Just 'out of the blue', Reverend Della, I don't know how and where it came from, but I got the money to do what I needed and there is even some to spare."

What do you mean out of the blue, what blue? You've been trying to reach God about this for the longest time and we finally prayed your way through and you make an out of the blue excuse.

Excuses will deceive you that you cannot do what you are totally equipped to do... and excuses make you fail. They give you a way (you think) to avoid the greater responsibility, which leads to the greater prize and the greater victory.

An excuse for a limited time, hear me good now, for that space in time will let you move out of that path. But if this is to be, it will be and as you don't handle it right now, it gains momentum and size and will roll back on you and beat you to death.

If you have to deal with it, whatever it is, you have to deal with it!

So, if you deal with it now while it's fresh and young and small, you don't allow it to roll around and pick up some of that other dumb stuff you've done, and they all come back in on you in force.

You wonder why you fail to get money. Excuses and "what ifs." "Oh, I can't do that," "Oh, that costs too much," "There is not enough 'cause times are hard, the economy is so bad."

Whatever you believe is true is true for you. People all around you are doing and buying and fulfilling dreams and having prayers answered.

You see a car and it is your dream car, the one you've been praying for. You go into the dealership and the man in the store has not asked you for a dime (this is about your prayer and your dream). You say, "This is a good looking car. I really like this car, um, how much does this car cost?" The man answers, "$70,000." And you respond, "Seventy thousand... seventy thousand? I could pay down on a house for that much money."

You went in there to see about a car. They don't sell houses in there.

The price becomes the excuse to keep from getting up and taking the responsibility of getting this down payment and these notes. You have this wonderful word rationalization, which means in essence, "I know this isn't true but I'm trying to make myself believe that it is."

You want money... you pray, "Lord, I need some money. Father, I need some money." Fourteen cents is "some money".

You need a vaccination from excusitis. Faith is that vaccination. Love of God is the bandage to cover the spot. Strength will come as the vaccination heals and you will benefit from the wisdom you have learned in your healing and you will become well enough to use your power to have and do and be and receive whatever you need or desire.

Stop using your illness for an excuse. Don't talk about your ailment... don't talk about the flu... because your power is in here, your throat and whatever you give credulousness to becomes stronger. Don't make illness your main topic of conversation. Talking about your health is a bad habit... it bores people... and it makes you seem self-centered.

No, I do not want to see your scar from your operation. No, I don't want to do that and I don't want to talk about your gallstones. If that's all you want to talk about, let's just sit here in the silence and praise God.

I don't need gallstones in my life. I don't have them but I am going to sit here and use my power to create them. Not hardly, I don't think so.

Stop complaining and thank God for whatever health you have. While you have read this chapter, many people have died and they no longer have any health at all. So whatever health you have, thank God for it.

I know there is no separation between me and my Father who is God the good.

I don't need excuses. For all that the Father is I am, and all that the Father has is mine. His omniscience (all of His knowledge), His omnipresence (evenly spread around me at all times), His omnipotence (His mighty power available for my use).

This is why you can go forward bravely. I don't have the excuse that my job doesn't pay enough. I am not counting on my job anyway. I'm expecting from my source God, and I am expecting the unexpected, which can be bigger than this room.

God can supply me with this room full of money so I open my mind. I'm ready to receive the expected and the unexpected, because I know there is nothing separating me from my Father and my Father is a good and loving Father.

He's omnipotent. He has all the power and He is omnipresent, evenly present. Wherever I am, God is, so I don't have any use for excuses to hide behind.

I'm standing on the rock that is a true foundation. I don't have to hide.

Say this aloud to yourself:

I make great choices, not excuses. I am expecting the unexpected.

(Again)

I make great choices, not excuses. I am expecting the unexpected.

I open my mind to receive the expected and the unexpected.

Father, I know you play no favorites. I am your child and I am worthy to receive prosperity. I know this to be the truth because you told me so.

Listen to what you've said. I am worthy... I am the child of God... I am God's child... I am worthy of prosperity!

"Well, you don't know what I've done, Rev. Della."

God knows what you've done. And let me tell you something that might surprise you. He doesn't care! You're the one who is worried about it. He forgave you

83

long ago. You just want to hold onto it for an excuse.

David said God's eyes are too pure to see the junk we do.

Say this aloud to yourself:

I withdraw any negative thoughts of excuses, any negative feelings of excuses on all levels of my life.
(Again)

If troubles or challenges appear, I know it is temporary. I don't dwell on it; I don't try to explain it. I am not frightened by it so I don't need excuses to hide behind.

I make choices, not excuse. I make choices, not excuses. I realize I cannot force my good, but I can invite my good into my life by faith, and by dwelling upon my good. I attract only my good in the name and the nature of Christ Jesus.

Wisdom

The dictionary says wisdom is: understanding what is true, right and lasting.

It is common sense, good judgment.

As a descriptive sentence, it said, "It is the characteristic of wisdom not to do desperate things."

Desperate things are reckless things, violent things done because of despair and suffering from unbearable needs and anxieties.

Metaphysically, wisdom is the ability to use knowledge with the attributes that come from the Christ within.

It is intuitive knowing: spiritual intuition.

The voice of God within us as the source of our understanding; mental actions based on the Christ truth within.

This knowing capacity transcends intellectual knowledge.

Spiritual discernment always places wisdom above the other faculties of the mind, revealing knowledge and intelligence, which are auxiliaries to understanding.

What you need to understand is your wisdom. If you feel you don't have much or any at all, we are going to see what you are willing to do about it.

First let's get some authority on the subject of wisdom. We'll go to Proverbs because the key word in Proverbs is wisdom, the ability to live life skillfully.

A Godly life in an ungodly world is no simple assignment.

Proverbs provides God's detailed instructions for His people to deal successfully with the practical affairs of everyday life.

Proverbs is one of the few Biblical books that clearly spells out its purpose.

Proverbs 4:7-8 *"Wisdom is the principle thing, therefore get wisdom; and in all your getting, get understanding. Exalt her, and she shall promote thee; she shall bring thee to honour when you embrace her."*

Embracing understanding is the end of confusion.

Wisdom is the partner of understanding.

With the wisdom of the Christ within, you get a much better understanding.

Proverbs 1:7 *"The fear* (respect) *of the Lord is the beginning of knowledge, but fools despise wisdom and instruction."*

Proverbs 19:8 *"He that gets wisdom loves his soul."*

WISDOM

Proverbs 16:16 *"How much better is it to get wisdom than gold."*

James 3:17 *"Wisdom from above is first pure, then peaceable, gentle, and easy to be entreated* (to entreat is to ask for something earnestly), *full of mercy and good fruits, without partiality and without hypocrisy."*

James 1:5-6 *"If any of you lack wisdom, let him or her ask of God, that giveth to all men and women liberally, unbraideth not* (won't tear you down or apart because you don't know) *and it shall be given him or her. But let him or her ask in faith, nothing wavering. For he that wavers is like waves of the sea driven with the wind and tossed."*

The gospel, the word of God is heavenly wisdom.

I Corinthians 2:5-7, 9 *"Your faith should not be in the wisdom of men but in the power of God.*

However, we speak wisdom among those who are mature, yet not the wisdom of this age, nor of the rulers of this age, who are coming to nothing.

But we speak the wisdom of God in a mystery, the hidden wisdom which God ordained before the ages for our glory."

But as it is written:

"Eye has not seen, nor ear heard, nor have entered into the heart of man the things which God has prepared for those who love Him."

You need to know this, when things need to be handled, be wise enough to go to the Christ inside of you.

For there are ways and means available to you that

87

He has prepared for you, "if" you love Him, that no one has seen or heard of! They are, "For your eyes only and for your ears only."

It is true that God is integrity.

It is true that He loves you and designed the life of abundance for you.

It is the right thing to believe.

It always has been true and it always will be true.

We can be at peace for God is in charge and all is well and well indeed."

We used to say in our Responsive Reading of Power, "We go forth with enthusiasm, excitement and expectancy." Expectancy from whom?

Why are we so excited and enthusiastic about this expecting thing?

To expect is to look forward to the probable occurrence or appearance of... to consider likely or certain... to consider reasonable or due.

The question is "What do you expect and who do you expect it from?"

How wise are your expectations?

Know this for sure right now, in order for someone or something to be able to fulfill your expectations, they must have the ability to do all that is required for success.

Let's see what you are willing to do about understanding your wisdom.

Are you wise enough, to trust God enough, to

place whatever needs repair in your life in the hands of God and get out of the way so He can fix it?

Are you wise enough to know intuitively that God wouldn't lie to you because He doesn't have to?

Because you hold no power over Him and therefore you are no threat to Him at all, so He has no need to lie to you.

He has told you He loves you and it is His great pleasure to give you the kingdom. Are you wise enough to really accept that as your truth?

Are you wise enough to accept that you are the salt of the earth and you cannot afford to lose your savor, because if you do, you lose your seasoning power and you're good for nothing, that's when life is able to throw you out and trample you under foot?

Some of your relationships, jobs, money, affairs have lost their savor.

Are you wise enough to be consciously aware that you are the light of the world and you have to let your light shine and not hide it under a bushel, but shine it from the highest hill?

Are you wise enough not to be liable for judgment by refusing and refuting anger and insults, gossip and lies?

Or, do you let it take you away from what you know is for your highest good?

Do you let things stop your clear thinking, leading you to a place where you encounter heart attacks and stomach ulcers, and other conditions bad for your body and mind and being?

WISDOM

Are you wise enough, to be strong enough, to just say yes when you mean yes and no when you mean no?

Or, do you have so little faith in the validity of your words, you feel the need to validate your word by swearing before God, or on your mama's grave or head or whatever? Or is it that you know you're lying?

Are you wise enough to know that vengeance is God's?

Or are you an eye for an eye and a tooth for a tooth person?

Are you wise enough not to resist the evildoer, not to be concerned with him or her at all because you know:

† The law that what you sow you are going to reap is active and effective always in all ways.

† What you have your attention on has its attention on you.

Are you wise enough to be receiving your loving rewards?

Are you being perfect as your Father is perfect and loving everybody so deeply that you include your enemies?

Are you wise enough to keep your eye single and on Him to keep it healthy and therefore, keep your whole body healthy and full of light?

Are you wise enough to be serving only one master?

Or are you serving your job and your house and your bank account, your mama, your husband, your wife, your children, your neighbors' opinions and what is politically correct?

Are you doing unto others as you would have them do unto you? Or do you feel you have to do others before they do you?

Are you wise enough to know that tomorrow will bring its own worries, and that today's trouble is enough for today and neither one of them (today or tomorrow) is worth worrying about because worry does not solve situations or conditions?

Or do you spend, or should I say, waste your time worrying about whatever it is, instead of getting to God and handling it and getting on with your life? Are you wise enough to be a good tree bearing good fruit or are you a tree that does not bear good fruit and should be cut down and thrown into the fire?

Are you wise enough to bring forth your good constantly because you know the secret that giving is the first step toward receiving?

Or are you holding onto your meager hoarded stash?

It is time to make your ears attentive to wisdom and incline your heart to understanding.

The Book of Proverbs gives us this priceless information.

Proverbs 2:10-11 *"When wisdom enters your heart, and knowledge is pleasant to your soul, discretion will preserve you and understanding will keep you."*

"God gives wisdom; from His mouth comes knowledge and understanding; He stores up sound wisdom for the upright.

WISDOM

With God wisdom will come into your heart and knowledge will be pleasant to your soul.

Happy are those who find wisdom, that those who get understanding, for her income is better than silver and her revenue better than gold.

She is more precious than jewels, and nothing you desire can compare with her. Long life is in her right hand; in her left hand are riches and honor. Her ways are ways of pleasantness, and all her paths are peace.

She is a tree of life to those who lay hold of her; those who hold fast are called happy."

The way we attain or acquire this wisdom is to let go of the personal self with its limited beliefs and take on the vastness of the Christ mind.

> I promise God and myself from this moment on; I will do all that is in my power to take only the good from each experience.

With What Measure You Mete

Matthew 7:1-5 *"Judge not, that ye be not judged. For with what judgment ye judge, ye shall be judged; and with what measure ye mete, it shall be measured to you again.*

And why beholdest thou the mote that is in thy brother's eye, but considerest not the beam that is in thine own eye?

Or how wilt thou say to thy brother, let me pull out the mote out of thine eye; and behold a beam is in thine own eye:

Thy hypocrite, first cast out the beam out of thine own eye and then shalt thou see clearly to cast out the mote out of thy brother's eye."

These five short verses, which are only about 100 words, are the most staggering document ever presented to mankind.

They deal with both the nature of man and the importance of his conduct for his own good, thereby making it good for all that surround him or her.

It is the true art of living and the secret of happiness and success.

When you really understand this document and believe it to be true, you will immediately revolutionize your whole life from top to bottom.

These verses express the simple and inescapable law of life. The plain fact is that it is the law of life. As we think and speak and act toward others, so will others think, speak and act toward us.

The law of retribution is a cosmic law, impersonal and unchanging just like the law of gravity; neither law considers or respects persons.

This law works without bitter, long lasting resentment or deep-seated ills, but also without pity, concern or favor.

Therefore it behooves us to think twice or more times before we treat other people unjustly.

This should cure you of looking for gratitude for what you do and it should stop you from complaining of ingratitude on the part of those you help.

You should help others for the true reason, that it is our duty to help others so far as we can do so wisely.

Doing your duty or giving should be its own reward, remembering that in some other way, the deed will surely be recognized and repaid, by the law of God, who can give you more than anybody, anyway!

When you look for gratitude, you are putting the other person under a sense of obligation. The person will probably get the message subconsciously, and resent it strongly.

You must learn to do your good deeds and then pass on, neither expecting nor wishing for personal recognition. For some of us that's hard! But know this:

The errors of thought, word and deed are worked out and satisfied under the law; but the good goes on forever, unchanging and undiminished by time.

It is in the realm of thought, that the law finds its true application. The one thing that matters, in the long run, is to keep your thoughts right about other people and about yourself. More than anything else, about yourself.

You need to keep the right thoughts about God, about your fellow man, and about yourself.

You need to know that dominion is located in the secret place of the most high.

The secret place you will focus your attention on is observing the commandment not to judge.

Some of you are saying, "These things are happening to me because of my karma."

The law of karma has no respect of persons, and forgets nothing. It is actually a law for matter and mind only. It is not the law of the spirit.

In spirit, all is perfect and eternal, unchangingly good. In spirit, there is no bad karma to be reaped, because none can be sown.

Through prayer and meditation, or as some of you refer to, as treatment, we transfer our attention to the domain of spirit.

So when we come to that extent under the law of perfect good, karma is wiped out.

So we have a choice between karma and Christ.

This is our charter of freedom, our dominion over all things; we are made in the image likeness of God. We have a choice.

We can remain in the limited regions of matter and mind or we can appeal through prayer to the reality of spirit, that is the Christ indwelling in us and be free.

When you understand rightly the Gospel of the Christ, you can and will be free. As soon as you pray, you begin to rise above karma.

When you practice the presence of God by praying, which is communing with God, there is no evil that the healing Christ will not destroy.

John 3:16-17 *"God so loved the world that He gave His only begotten son, that whosoever believed in Him should not perish but have everlasting life.*

God sent not His son into the world to condemn the world; but that the world through Him might be saved."

Let's break that statement down.

God so loved the world that He manifested Himself, as His unique Christ power, so that whosoever chooses this Christ power, shall not perish through His own weakness or frailty, but shall have everlasting salvation.

When sufficient prayer or meditation has been done, the sinner (mistake maker) becomes a changed person, and will not even desire to repeat His mistakes, then He is saved and the penalties are remitted for Christ is Lord of all, karma included.

The higher law of spirit overrides or supersedes all the lower laws of the physical man's mental planes. You, because of your essential given selfhood, have the power of rising above all domains into the infinite dimension of spirit, where such laws no longer affect you.

It is not that you have broken the laws, it is that you have ventured beyond them.

You have gone into the Christ that is inside of you and you reside there in the peace that surpasses all human understanding.

You are the greatest thing that God has made. I am not making it up. He said so! He made you in His image-likeness that you are able to do, to have and be all that you desire to do, have, and be, that is for your highest good! We are able to do this but we don't always do the things we are able to do.

Instead, we seem to be satisfied doing the smallest, smuttiest, non beneficial things.

You need to help yourself. Get the beam out of your eye and the speck in your brother's eye may just be something you see because your beam is distorting your vision.

If that is not the case, get your eye clear enough to help your brother or sister without trying to bind them with your need for gratification and appreciation.

God is constantly aware of every blessing you give. He is the one that will see to it that you get just what you deserve and the accurate amount that you deserve returned to you.

Galatians 6:7-10 *"Be not deceived; God is not mocked; for whatsoever a man soweth, that shall he also reap. For he that soweth to his flesh shall of the flesh* *reap corruption;*

But he that soweth to the spirit shall of the spirit reap life everlasting. And let us not be weary in well doing; for in due season we shall reap, if we faint not. As we have therefore opportunity, let us do good unto all men, especially unto them who are of the household of faith."

This applies to women also!

God is infinite Love.

I give great measures of Love.

Infinite Love is the only cause, the only activity and the only measure I mete therefore, Love is returned to me as the most prominent experience in my life.

Power

The word of God is His creative power. It includes all the potentialities of being life, wisdom, substance, power, strength. All of God's other attributes.

All who have faith in its power to accomplish that whereto it is sent, may speak the word with effect.

The word I want to speak about now is power.

Your power is given to you by God for your use, for your highest good.

What is power and much more importantly, what is your power?

Power: the ability to do or act; it is great or marked ability to do or act; strength, might, force, possession or control, authority, one who possesses or exercises authority.

Metaphysically speaking, our power consists of 5 tools that we work with.

† Faith in God and in you

† Confidence in God and you

POWER

† Interest in God and in you

† Mastery through God to you

† Dedication to God and you

Your power is God through you. You are your power.

When you know your oneness with the omnipotence of God, then learning to contact this inner power and to keep that inner power flowing recharges you. It is like an electrical current.

You have spiritual power, mental power, physical power, material power.

We cultivate the physical and some cultivate the mental. All of us need to cultivate the spiritual power.

The five steps to spiritual power are:

† Unity. Oneness with God.

† Vision. The ability to see God in all things.

† Devotion. To God in all His forms.

† Joy. To give and to receive.

† Release. To rid oneself of things no longer for our highest good.

Our power is innate control over our thoughts and feelings.

It is a quickening from on high that must precede our realization of our dominion.

Acts 1:8 "*You shall receive power, when the Holy*

POWER

Spirit is come upon you. "

God is all power and therefore all things are possible with Him.

Your mind and your body have power to transform energy from one plane of consciousness to another.

From God through you to you. This is the power and dominion implanted in us from the beginning of time.

A powerful person is one who possesses and exercises authority or influence; one who has great effectiveness.

Power is my ability to change and build consciousness.

Power is my ability to choose my thoughts and feelings.

Power is my ability to transform energy from one plane to another.

What does that mean, Rev. Della?

In its simple explanation, I can and so can you, raise the level of my consciousness and move my energy from defeat to success, from sickness to health, from loneliness to happiness.

I can exalt my ideas and my ideals and change my life from the basement to the penthouse.

I have just given you great power. I have given you truthful information.

Information is power.

Here is some even greater power. Every attribute

of God is an attribute of man because man is made in the image likeness of his Father.

Each attribute that God has implanted in you is an ability you have with which to build consciousness.

In consciousness development, you need the use of your ability to move spiritual energy about.

To do so, you must rid yourself of certain characteristics and add new ones.

To start with, you need to be able to tell the truth to you and to everybody else.

You need to accept your power which will enable you to remove your fear.

You need to increase your "be with God time", and completely destroy "what if" and "I wonder" with your power to "know that you know what you know".

You need to become involved in action and move away from procrastination.

Increase your consciousness and increase your power.

God is absolute power and your ability to draw upon God as power allows you to transform solids into liquids, ideas into bridges, and thoughts into buildings.

God power is your ability to heal. Change your environment and draw your good to you.

Power when it is realized within and accepted in consciousness, is divine energy and it rearranges itself to form into outer manifestations according to the new inner realization.

POWER

Our gift of power is quickened through mental contact with the source, which I hasten to add is silence.

Pure power is silence, just as strength is stillness, power is silence. Strength is expended when you convert it into movement and action. Power is expended when you convert it into vibrations or the word.

When you speak the word, you name the form which spirit will take. The creation was done with:

"And God said."

Divine energy becomes anything you come to believe so it is important to watch your thoughts, belief, and words very carefully because you are building or tearing down your consciousness through the power you give to them.

The stages of power in action are:

† Silence

† Thought

† The spoken word

† Manifestation

In the silence there is no vibration. It is just God as absolute power.

It awaits your need to be recognized by you.

As you draw on the silence, a thought enters your head and it registers in your consciousness as a vibration.

The lower the frequency of the vibration, the more pure the thought is for it is "the still small voice."

The rate of vibrations is determined by your

consciousness, and your spiritual development.

This is why meditation and relaxation are so closely aligned.

The lowering of your thought waves elevates your creativity and spiritual awareness.

Anger and fear throw you into a very high pitch while love and assurance lower the level of vibrations.

That is the reason when you run around like a chicken with its head cut off, you can't get anything done.

After a thought enters your head, you direct it by speaking the word.

Silence is your pure power. Thought is your formed power. The word is your expressed power which becomes manifest.

It is vital that you realize what you are doing when you send your thoughts forth into the world, into the pit of race consciousness. I mean the human race consciousness.

You are literally shaping and forming the conditions in which you live.

According to your consciousness, your world is being sustained.

What to do, what to do?

You can change your environment and the world around you by elevating your thinking, and by watching your mouth. Most of you don't know where your power is! It is in your throat. It is in your words. It's in what you say. All your words create.

That should frighten you so badly. Just think of some of the things you have said in just the last 24 hours. You spoke it but you don't want it.

The society in which we live expects a large amount of glibness, superficial, insincere wittiness and we say things we really don't need in our lives in order to please the audience.

Your thoughts create things, but you speak them into existence. Every word you speak of lack is a false image, a mental image and you give it strength through your persistent thought, and then you speak that false image into existence and you fortify it with constant discussion.

What do I mean?

The contract, The Bible, says watch your words with all diligence, because you are continually reaping the fruits of your words.

You see, whatever you say is, in your life it is.

Whatever it is.

If you start right now saying, "I'm powerful!" and "I'm magnificent!" and "I'm drawing to me all the things I want, need, desire, feel like I want to have, that is for my highest good", and you believe that and you constantly say that, stuff will start jumping from behind bushes for you.

You already know the process works because you've been using it but in the wrong direction.

You've been telling yourself "there is no way out" and "they keep holding you back" and "the economy won't allow you to prosper," and that is exactly what has been happening to you, and that more abundantly.

You've been saying that to you! If you hadn't been saying that to you, and you hadn't believed it, it wouldn't be taking place in your life today.

You brought that into your life. Because you have this power!

Whether you use it right or not, you have the power.

Jeremiah 23:36 *"Every man's word shall be his burden."*

Job 22:28 *"Thou shall also decree a thing and it shall be established unto you."*

You need to speak to your problems. You need to speak to your pain. You need to speak to all those things that are keeping you from living the God life of prosperity and abundance that you should lead. You should speak to them now with power.

Because your spoken word hammers the thing you desire into shape. It then forms the visible substance in accordance with the picture that you have in your mind. So you would do yourself some good to just sit down and be with God and create what you want.

Nothing comes into your life uninvited. You invite it with your thoughts and with your words.

James 3:2-10, 13-14 *"For in many things we offend all. If any man offend not in word, then he is a perfect man, and able also to bridle the whole body.*

Behold we put bits into the horses' mouth that they may obey us; and we turn about their whole body.

Behold also the ships, which though they be so great and are driven of fierce winds, yet they are turned

106

about with a very small helm, whithersoever the governor listeth.

Even so the tongue is a little member, and boast great things. Behold, how great a matter a little fire kindles.

The tongue is a fire, a world of iniquity; so is the tongue among our members, that it defiles the whole body, and sets on fire the course of mature; and it is set on-the-fire of hell.

For every kind of beast and bird and serpent or things in the sea, is tamed, and hath been tamed by mankind.

But the tongue can no man tame; it is an unruly evil, full of deadly poison.

With the tongue we bless God, even the Father; and with the tongue we curse men, which are made after the similitude of God.

Out of the same mouth proceeds blessings and cursing. My brothers these things ought not to be so.

Who is a wise man and endued with knowledge among you? Let him shew out of a good conversation his works with meekness of wisdom.

The wisdom that is from above is first pure, then peaceable, gentle, and easy to entreated, full of mercy and good fruits, without partiality, and without hypocrisy. "

Faith controls the tongue, and we must learn to speak the word. We must confidently affirm the word.

Sit down, put your feet flat on the floor, and concentrate on this:

Father, let the words of my mouth and the meditations of my heart be acceptable in thy sight.

Lord, teach me how to serve thee. Lord, teach me how to pray.

I do not accept this appearance in my life, in my health, in my wealth, in my happiness, in my world or in my affairs. No! I don't accept this! No! I do not accept this.

I am the King's kid and my Father's desire and plan for me is what I deserve, the very best. Therefore I will accept only the very best.

In the name of Christ Jesus I accept this is my truth and so it is and Amen.

Spiritual Power

Acts 1:5 *"For John truly baptized with water; but you shall be baptized with the Holy Ghost not many days hence."*

Acts 1:8 *"But you shall receive power, after that the Holy Ghost is come upon you; and ye shall witnesses unto me both in Jerusalem and in Judea and in Samaria, and unto the uttermost part of the Earth."*

Let's start in Jerusalem (in peace) and in Judea (in praise) and in Samaria (a watch tower) and open ourselves for the Father visited upon us His whole, the Holy Ghost.

Now we have power.

What kind of power?

Activated power.

There are these powers that are ours.

† Spiritual power

† Mental power

† Emotional power

SPIRITUAL POWER

† Physical power

† Material power

Faith is our highest power because it connects us to spiritual power.

Confidence in yourself is a spiritual power!

You are the power, activated by God Himself.

When you use your personal power constructively, you will be in a proper relationship with:

† God

† With life

† With yourself

† Other people

† With your work

† With the manifestation of your dreams.

You need to learn and know yourself on these five levels of consciousness and put these five keys for manifestation into effect in your life.

You have to:

† Reorganize

† Visualize

† Energize

† Realize

† Actualize your personal power

And not necessarily in that order.

Spiritual power is the source of all things.

Spiritual power is life power. Spirit is God within us. Spirit must be used. It is eternal and enduring. Spirit is what we really are. It is our higher self.

Spirit includes everything. That is why we start with it.

Spirit is God's first gift to us but we have forgotten it.

Genesis 2:7 *"And God breathed into him the breath of life."* The root word for breath is spirit.

And God breathed into him the spirit of life.

Everyday when you inhale you inspire and when you exhale or breathe out you expire. Expire is also used when a person dies, it is when the spirit leaves the body.

When we have true spiritual power, all the rest will automatically follow. That is why Jesus told us to, *"Seek ye first the kingdom of Heaven and all these things will be added unto you."*

You must realize that you are one with the source of all power.

You have to learn to see the larger picture, the larger scope, of things.

Give up pettiness. Become devoted to life. Devotion is love, praise and worship of the wonder of life.

Become joyful. Let the magnificence and beauty of life fill you to overflowing.

111

Release that other stuff.

Let the unobstructed flow of life fill you and work through you to you.

There is no place where God leaves off and you begin, and visa versa!

I repeat, there is no place where God leaves off and you begin and visa versa!

You are a cell in the Great Spirit... the Great Mind... the Great Body of God!

There is only one power and one presence in the universe and that power and that presence is God the good, omnipotent (all power), omniscient (all the knowledge) and omnipresent (evenly present). Become aware of this magnificent potential within yourself.

Learn not to even try to do anything yourself. Let the spiritual power do it through you.

Jesus talking, *"The Father that dwells in me, He does the works."*

Correct your vision, watch where you look and you can have as far as you can see.

If you can only see the small and disparaging, you can only receive the small and disparaging.

Emerson, a great metaphysician, said, "Contemplate the facts of life from the highest point of view."

Remove the beam from your eye and stop worrying about the speck in everyone else's eye.

Matthew 6:22 *"If therefore thine eye be single,*

thy whole body shall be full of light."

Spiritual power is the direct result of our worship.

Worship is the process of living, praising and blessing our oneness with God.

Contacting and unifying with the higher self, which is the spirit within you. Fall in love with the infinite goodness of God and give your entire self to that goodness.

Surrender completely.

Give thanks to the source from which all good comes.

Praise God from whom all blessings flow!

Praise the creative power, which produces all things.

Adore the very idea of life.

Devote yourself to serving the good, the true and the beautiful.

Remember how your mother or grandmother or aunt used to hum all the time? Sing your praises, let your joy be unrestrained.

Laugh every chance you get. Let your laughter ring out. Let yourself overflow with good will. Stop being so sad, mad and bored.

Life is a ball. Get interested in everyone and everything.

Let your excitement, your interest and enthusiasm color everything you do.

Infect others with your joyousness.

Whatever you do, do it joyfully.

Stop struggling and straining and let concern go out of your life.

You are the power, and the power works through you.

Just as you need God, and you really do, God needs you to work His power through.

Get in tune with the spirit within you. Unify with it. Know what you want to accomplish, then let the spiritual power produce it for you.

There will be work for you to do. But your work will be guided by God, who knows the correct procedure, and how to proceed constructively.

Worry is not constructive. Jesus talking, *"Therefore take no thought, saying what shall we eat; or what shall we drink? Or wherewithal shall we be clothed? The Father knows what things you have need of before you ask Him."* **Matthew 6:31-32**

Our job is "what", God's job is how!

Let the spirit inspire you, then let it flow through you and do the job. Develop these steps and you will be able to effectively use the spiritual power that is yours.

When you get organized, when you begin to visualize, let the spirit energize, because once you really realize, you can actualize your personal power to master your life, your world, and your affairs.

I am one with all the power there is.
(Feel that!)

I will learn how to contact His power within me!
(Think about that)

I will learn how to cooperate with this power!
(Promise this sincerely to yourself)

I will learn how to use this power wisely.

I will keep this power flowing. If I will do this, nothing will be impossible for me!

Understanding
Our Spiritual Power

The truth, and the principles, which are the truth, absolutely works. No matter the name, nature or seeming extreme power of your needs, desires, situations or circumstances.

How many of you are aware that God is consciously aware of you and your needs and He stands ever ready, and absolutely able to service you?

I love thinking that, I love knowing that, I love the sound of that, my Father, God, and my Brother, Christ Jesus, want to service me.

Service as you know, are acts of assistance, benefits, favors and devotion.

Some of you already know what I am going to say next because you have tried Him and He has brought you through; but for those of you who may not know it, I am a witness, and you can believe me, the system works! We just have to understand it and apply it.

2 Timothy 1:7 *"For God has not given us the spirit of fear. God has given us the spirit of power, and of love, and of sound mind."*

Spirit is the principle of animation. It is a prompting action. Let's take it from the top.

Genesis 2:7 *"And the Lord God formed man off the dust of the ground, and breathed into his nostrils the breath of life; and man became a living soul."*

God breathed into us, the spirit of life and we were animated.

Until He breathed the spirit of life into us, we were just dust.

We are made in God's image likeness, we too have the creative power to create from the dust, our desires, our dreams, and our needs, and blow into them the spirit of life and animate them.

Spirit and breath come from the same root word spīritus.

Spirit is Jesus' gift to us.

John 16:7 *"Nevertheless I tell you the truth, it is expedient for you that I go away; for if I go not away, the comforter will not come unto you. But if I depart, I will send Him unto you"*

John 16:13 *"How be it when He, the spirit of truth, is come, He will guide you into all truth;"*

John 14:16-17 *"And I will pray the Father, and He shall give you another comforter, that He may abide with you forever; even the spirit of truth; whom the world cannot receive, because it seeth Him not; neither knoweth Him; but you know Him; for He dwelleth with you, and shall be in you."*

John 14:18 *"I will not leave you comfortless. I*

117

will come to you. "

Spirit is a principle or, if you will, an attitude that inspires. It animates thoughts, feelings, and actions. The Holy Spirit is the executive power, of both the Father and the Son.

Executive = management and authority and administration.

An executor is one appointed by a testator, one who has made a legally, valid will before his death.

Jesus is the testator and the Holy Spirit appointed by Jesus is the executor.

Jesus gave us the comforter, which is the Holy Spirit.

He gave us the right to ask in His name believing as we pray, and we shall have whatsoever we desire that is for our highest good.

We must understand this.

The Holy Spirit carries out the creative plan. It is sent out to do definite works. It speaks for us. It searches out what we need to do, what we have to do. It reveals knowledge, information and instructions.

We are constantly in a place where we need to use the benefits of the Holy Spirit.

Have you got this so far?

In order to use the benefits of the Holy Spirit, we must believe that:

† God is integrity, unimpaired, completeness, with rigid

adherence to a code of absolute good behavior.

† It is impossible for God to lie to us. It is against His nature of absolute good.

† What God said is true! It has always been true and it will always be true.

† We need to have faith enough to stand on God's truth.

† We need to love God enough to be at peace with that truth.

† We need to be strong enough in that truth.

† To be wise enough in that truth to use the power of the Holy Spirit based on the truth.

You got that part?

What is my point?

You must understand how powerful you really are and use that power in the name and nature of Christ Jesus.

Philippians 2:5-6 *"Let this mind be in you which was also in Christ Jesus; who being in the form of God, thought it not robbery to be equal with God."*

Understand that you can breathe into your life, your desires, your dreams, your relationships, your future, this spirit of life and activate them.

Become aware of your asking power in Jesus' name.

Be willing to learn how to use your executive power.

119

God is all there is in the Universe and in my life.

There is ONLY GOD. There is NOTHING but GOD.

I GIVE NO POWER TO ANYTHING BUT GOD IN MY LIFE.

Emotional Power

Have you ever kept track of yourself as you tried to keep the negative from distracting you?

I am willing to wager that the thing that threw you off the farthest was an emotional thing.

Unexpected and emotional.

How about that?

You never really know a thing until you can respond to it emotionally.

Feeling is the secret to responding.

Thought cannot come to life until you respond to it.

Because thought must be fertilized by feeling.

Thought plus feeling brings about conviction.

Conviction produces results.

Clarity of thought plus intensity of feelings are the twin keys to personal power.

Of course these keys must be used through your spiritual powers.

Haven't you noticed the person who feels deeply invariably is filled with emotional energy and personal power?

Energy and power are released through the emotional nature.

Because our emotions are, the motors which run the machine.

Uncontrolled emotions vibrate destructively and produce weakness, confusion, sickness, pain and embarrassment.

When your emotions are controlled and used correctly your emotions are the manufacturing plant for health, happiness, success and achievement.

Your emotional power can make you or break you. Your thoughts provide the plan through the conscious mind and your emotions are the powers, which produce, from that plan.

There are many feelings, desires, urges, drives and motives working in our emotional field.

We may not ever understand them all or even recognize them all because we have so much emotional power and such a large emotional field.

But we certainly can learn to control them through unconditional love.

Love among many, many other things is affirmative emotional attachment to an idea. Love is the longing of life to express itself.

That's what we are. God's longing to express life.

Love really does make the world go around for God is love and God makes the world go around.

Love is the one supreme emotional feeling.

Matthew 19:26 *"With God all things are possible."*

With love all things are possible.

Love is not only the cement, the holding harmonizing cement to your relationships, it is the cement to your ideas and your dreams.

Love is the divine ingredient that unifies us with all living things and all things necessary to make our desires and dreams realities.

To have abundance or prosperity we must first love God and feel that love.

We must love our neighbors as ourselves.

Therein lies the rub. Most of you don't really love yourselves. You are forever putting you down. You are not consciously aware of the wondrousness in your real self so you can't respond to something you don't know even exists.

Therefore you love your neighbor the same way by putting him down and not even recognizing his or her wondrousness, because you don't know it exists. We judge others by ourselves.

Our next step is Faith.

Faith is the substance of things hoped for and the evidence of things not seen.

Faith is knowing, believing, trusting. It is reliance and conviction. These are all aspects of faith.

Faith gives you confidence in yourself and what you are doing or dreaming or planning.

Faith is the first ingredient to success.

Trust and use the power within you so as to be able to go all the way with your ideas.

Faith allows you to replace fears and negative emotions with love and assurance.

You should be consciously aware that authority springs from a strong inner faith.

It allows you to live in the assurance that all good things are waiting to happen to you.

In constant assurance that all things work together for the good of those who love the Lord.

Whatever you need done in your life, world or your affairs, can be done through the Christ inside you that strengthens you.

Spend a few moments in silence. Take a few deep breaths. Feed yourself these affirmations:

Whatever I need done in my life, world and affairs, I can do through the Christ inside me that strengthens me.

"The Lord is my shepherd (God is in charge of taking care of me).

I shall not want (all He is I am, all He has is mine).

He makes me lie down in green pastures (in the middle of this desert He has prepared this cool grassy place).

He leadeth me beside the still waters (I am with Him in this quiet restful place).

He restores my soul; He leads me in the path of righteousness (into right thinking followed by right actions).

For His name's sake (for He has given His word).

Yea though I walk through the valley of the shadow of death, I will fear no evil; for thou art with me;

Your rod (the power of the Christ in me, the "I Am" of dominion and mastery) *and your staff they comfort me* (My staff, is a stick carried for many purposes, walking, climbing, as weapon, carried as a symbol of authority).

God prepares a table before me in the presence of mine enemies; God anoints my head with oil and my cup runs over.

Surely goodness and mercy shall follow me all the days of my life (with You taking care of me like this, Father).

I will dwell in the house of The Lord forever."

Stop. Take a few more deep breaths before you go further.

EMOTIONAL POWER

Learn to feel as David did. Walk beside the still waters and lie down in the green pastures of the spirit. Rely completely on God.

Develop that inner serenity and tranquility which is the source of all power.

It is in your best interest never to react to the turbulence and confusion of outer activities.

This is not an easy thing to do but it is worth it, you will find you feel better for the doing of it.

Learn to act from your center of inner peace.

Let the storms rage and the winds blow and if they threaten you, from the peace in you command them to be still in the name of Jesus.

Jesus speaking, *"Peace I give unto you, not as the world gives, give I unto you. Let not your heart be troubled neither let it be afraid."* **John 14:27**

These are two killing things that Jesus was trying to save us from.

A troubled heart is worry in your subconscious mind, which causes fear, which makes you do things that burden your life.

He's telling us not to allow these things to take place in our lives through these emotional feelings.

The kingdom of peace is within each of us, we have but to go inside and get it.

We must maintain a balance between our thoughts and our feelings.

There must be a marriage between our intellect,

our intelligence and our feelings to produce right actions.

We use the term, "Father Mother God."

God is both intelligence and feelings. Executive power and nurturing.

We must get on the God beam and keep our thoughts and feelings under control and we must continuously examine our motives.

You must ask yourself:

Why do I feel this way so strongly?

Why am I letting (allowing) this to get me off my peaceful God beam?

Is this really worth my discontent?

We have to curb some of our urges and appetites and desires.

Be strong and definite in your feelings and attitudes but always suggest more that you actually express.

There are many ways to communicate your feelings, without saying words you cannot take back that put you in bondage.

Stay in the driver's seat, know who you are and be aware of what you are doing.

Do not allow yourself to be carried away by wrong thinking, feelings, people or things.

It's a big order but you and the calm peace of your soul and the ability to use your emotional power productively are worth a big order of procedure.

Catch fire with your ideas and your life and your world and your affairs. Stop panning and start praising.

Enthusiasm literally means, "Possessed by God."

Enthusiasm is contagious; it is spiritual, mental and emotional thrust.

With enthusiasm you can cut through countless difficulties.

Enthusiasm is interest and joy in action.

Enthusiasm releases your power potentiality, and it covers your world with a rosy hue.

It lifts you above the humdrum and commonplace.

It releases your power of expectancy.

It provides you with the vital and dynamic energy, which accomplishes all good things.

Enthusiasm is God in action through you, with God's power and love supporting you.

And your love of yourself and your neighbor.

And your faith and your enthusiasm for a peaceful productive life.

You cannot fail to get your emotion in a condition to be used powerfully and secure the calm peace of your soul.

Worry-Confidence-Courage

Worry as described in the Random House Dictionary: "To feel uneasy or anxious; to fret;

Torment oneself with or suffer from disturbing thoughts;

To move with effort; to make uneasy or anxious;

Trouble; torment with annoyances, cares, plague, pester or bother.

Anxious... Full of mental stress or uneasiness because of apprehension of danger or misfortune. Greatly worried.

Apprehension... The anticipation of adversity. Dread or fear of coming evil.

Worry is an inside job. You are responsible for it, because you feed it.

Worry would be unable to live without feeding it. Worry is not a reality, it is concocted.

For example, you say, "But I may lose my job."

The statement itself lets you know it's not real. Because as of yet, it has not happened. Fear is making you anticipate.

Worry is not required. It won't help you get your job back. It won't help you feel good about losing your job.

You are being apprehensive about it. So you set up the structure on how to draw that to you.

The more you worry about it, the more you begin to act like it, and accept that it is so.

If indeed you are going to lose your job, your thoughts should be on how to acquire a better one, with more permanency.

Worry is a waste of time and your creative energies.

1 Peter 5:7 *"Casting all your care upon Him; for He careth for you."*

John 14:1 *"Let not* (don't allow) *your heart be troubled; ye believe in God, believe also in Me."*

Philippians 4:6-7 *"Be careful of nothing; but in everything by prayer and supplication with thanksgiving let your request be made known unto God.*

And the peace of God, which passeth all understanding, shall keep your hearts and minds through Christ Jesus."

John 14:27 *"Peace I leave with you. My peace I give unto you not as the world giveth, give I unto you. Let not your heart be troubled, neither let it be afraid."*

So the need for worry does not exist.

Andre' Crouch wrote a song that I love called "I've Got Confidence".

"When trouble is in my way; I can't
tell the night from day; when I'm
tossed from side to side; like a ship
on a raging tide;

I don't worry, I don't fret; God has
never failed, yes; troubles come from
time to time; but that's all right I'm
not the worrying kind, cause

I've got confidence I know; God will
see me through; No matter what the
case may be;

I know He's gonna fix it for me

Some folks wonder how I smile;
even though I'm goin' through trials;
how can I have a song when
everything is going wrong; I don't
worry I don't fret;

God has never failed me yet.

Yeah troubles come from time to
time but that's all right; I am not the
worrying kind cause I've got
confidence God is gonna see me
through; no matter what the case
may be I know God will fix it for
me."

Confidence is full trust.   It is belief in the trustworthiness or reliability of a person or a thing. It is self-reliance,   assurance,   faith,   reliance, dependence, courage, trust.

It is reliance on integrity, reliance on strength, confident expectation of something or someone.

It is the certainty of future payment.

When you accept this truth as your truth, these promises of God should give you confidence, which is the beginning of the production of courage.

Courage according to the dictionary is the quality of mind or spirit that enables one to face difficulty, danger, pain, etc., with firmness and without fear;

It is bravery; to act in accordance with one's belief, in spite of criticism (the courage of one's conviction).

Deuteronomy 31:6 *"Be strong and of a good courage. Fear not, nor be afraid of them; for the Lord thy God, He it is that doth go with thee; He will not fail thee, nor forsake thee."*

Psalm 27:14 *"Wait on the Lord; be of good courage and He shall strengthen thy heart; wait I say upon the Lord."*

God's message through Joshua, we are Joshua.

Joshua 1:5-7 *"There shall not any man be able to stand before thee all the days of thy life; as I was with Moses, so will I be with thee; I will not fail thee nor forsake thee. Be strong and of a good courage."*

Psalm 62:1-2 *"Truly my soul waiteth upon God; from Him cometh my salvation.*

He only is my rock and my salvation; He is my

defense; I shall not be moved."

Psalm 27:1-3 *"The Lord is my light and my salvation; whom shall I fear? The Lord is the strength of my life; of whom shall I be afraid?*

Though a host should encamp against me, my heart shall not fear. Though war should rise against me, in this will I be confident."

You gain confidence and strength by every experience in which you really stop to look fear in the face.

You are able to say, "I lived through this horror, with God, and I can take the next thing that comes along. The Big Three and me are unbeatable.

Sooner or later we must all learn to stand alone, with God. Nothing else can make you master of your own destiny. God is the spring of all joy, comfort, power and courage.

We cannot escape adversity by running away and worrying about it as we hide in fear.

Sometimes you have to go through stuff to get to your stuff.

Take Joseph for an example. Joseph was Jacob's and Rachel's child of their old age. He was their twelfth son and Jacob loved him. He made him a coat of many colors.

Of course Joseph loved the coat and sported it around with pride, which of course he had the right to do.

His brothers hated that coat because to them, it was proof that Jacob loved Joseph more than he loved them. Plus Joseph was a dreamer, which they did not

134

understand at all.

So they decided to kill him. They beat him, tore up his coat, and threw him in a ditch half dead.

But his oldest brother didn't have the heart to kill him so they sold him to a caravan that came by going to Egypt, which is where his good was and the good of his father and his brothers. He went to jail, which was where he was discovered and presented to the Pharaoh, whom he helped to the extent that the Pharaoh made him second in command, second only to him.

Joseph went through some stuff to get to his stuff. Everything that seemed like a stumbling block was really a stepping-stone. Joseph didn't complain, doubt, or try to be anything but what he was. He believed in God so he leaned on God and trusted Him in the midst of all that happened to him and he got his abundance of stuff.

I find it most interesting that Joseph's name metaphysically means, "Whom Jehovah will add to; Jehovah shall increase; He shall increase progressively from perfection to perfection."

That was the level of Joseph's level of consciousness.

We know the level of his consciousness by his statement to his brothers.

Genesis 50:19-20 *"And Joseph said unto them, 'Fear not; for am I in the place of God? But as for you, ye thought evil against me; but God meant it unto good, to bring to pass, as it is this day to save much people alive.'"*

Life is consciousness and we cannot separate ourselves from our consciousness. You cannot rise above

135

your level of consciousness.

But you certainly can raise your level of consciousness. We must not be so aware of the challenge or condition or situation.

We must be still and become aware of God by directing our thinking and feelings toward God.

Rev up your love faculty and faith faculty.

Get in touch with your center. Become consciously aware of your Christ self, which is where you experience the presence of God. There, in the presence of God, lies your courage and your patience and your victory.

The thing that keeps us from having confidence is fear.

Fear destroys our courage and there is no confidence without courage.

It takes courage to serve God. It takes courage to have confidence.

Know this, really, really know this.

Fear is a fact and you must realize that in order to conquer it.

Fear is not a reality because fear is not of God. Only God is real.

It is not a reality because it has no power, other than the power you supply it with.

Most fear is psychological. A fear is capable of influencing your mind and your emotions. Worry, tension, embarrassment, panic all stem from mismanaged

136

negative imagination.

Action cures fear...did you hear me? Action cures fear.

When you face a tough problem you will stay mired in the mud until you take affirmative action.

Put your principles to work.

Whatever is happening to you has a reason. What is the cause? Fix the cause and the effects will have to stop for there will be nothing to feed the cause.

Hebrew 10:35-36 *"Cast not away therefore your confidence which hath great recompense of reward. For you have need of patience, that after you have done the will of God, you might receive the promise."*

Isaiah 43:2 *"When you pass through the waters* (emotions) *I will be with thee; and through the rivers, they shall not overflow thee; when you walk through the fire, you shall not be burned; neither shall the flame kindle upon you."*

1 John 5:14 *"And this is the confidence that we have in Him, that, if we ask anything according to His will, He heareth us."*

Proverbs 14:26 *"In fear* (respect) *of the Lord is strong confidence; and His children shall have a place of refuge."*

Hebrew 3:6 *"But Christ, as a Son, over His own house; in whose house we are, if we hold fast to the confidence and rejoicing of the hope* (faith) *firm unto the end."*

Don't be afraid; go on through this stuff because your real good stuff is on the other side of this stuff. You just have to know that God will never leave you nor forsake you, and that God is consciously aware of you, so you make sure you're consciously aware of God.

God has a way of taking what seems to be a big mistake and making a great miracle out of it.

As for us, we are inclined to get disappointments and appointments mixed up.

Walk away from your problem and let God work on the answer.

When you see what He comes up with, you will be glad you didn't try to work it out.

Life's answers are lost to us because we keep leaning on our own understanding, or taking advice from those who are as much in the dark as we are.

Proverbs 3:5-10 *"Trust in the Lord with all thine heart; and lean not unto thine own understanding.*

In all thy ways acknowledge Him, and He shall direct thy paths. Be not wise in thine own eyes; fear the Lord (respect the Lord) *and depart from evil.*

It shall be health to thy navel, and marrow to your bones.

Honor the Lord with thy substance, and with the first fruits of all thine increase; so shall thy barns be filled with plenty, and thy presses shall bust out with new wine."

I will be of good courage, and the Lord will strengthen my heart, bringing peace and comfort to my mind, and prosperity to my life.

Obedience

Do you remember when you were growing up how you vowed that when you got grown nobody was going to tell you what to do ever again?

I do and I took a lot of hard knocks because I just did not want anybody telling me what to do. I've still got some of that!

Obedience, the dictionary says, is to comply with or follow the commands, restriction, wishes or instructions of someone or something.

To submit or conform in action to some guiding principle.

We tend to think of obedience, only as a restriction, something forced upon us.

Therefore obedience is very difficult for some of us because we believe that obeying puts us under the power of someone else, or it is something that stops us from doing what we want to do.

Especially the things that are most enjoyable!

Obedience is entered into your computer (mind) that way from childhood, with "no's" and "don'ts" and spankings with some people beatings both physically and mentally.

You remember this forced obedience, the threatening, that fearful uncomfortable obedience.

Plus life has not granted the things you were told it would, if you obeyed.

Have you ever had cause to say or feel, "I did everything they told me, just like they told me, and it still doesn't work."?

So in your computer, obedience has a very volatile and hostile reaction.

You resent no matter how subtle those you have need to obey.

We have created in our ideas a God who is partial, subject to appeal from saint and sinner alike.

A God who can be persuaded or bargained with.

A God to who gives life and takes it away.

A God who heals sickness and causes it.

A God who impoverishes and enriches.

A God who rewards and punishes.

And having accepted these wrong ideas our prayers are largely a matter of doubts, and are lacking in that strong assurance that a thing will be, must be, shall be so, because it is in accordance to divine law, God's law.

Obedience.

To be obedient: is to be willing to obey, to submit

to one in authority.

It is conformity to the authority of a religious superior, especially on the part of one who has vowed such conformances to the ruler or authority.

We will obey some things easily. For an example, if you wish to start your car, you must obey the rules. You must first put the key in the ignition and turn it while accelerating the gas. To move it you must obey the rules by putting it in gear and so on.

The same is true with your spiritual car. You must obey.

Obedience is the governor of all movement whether it is mechanical, literal or spiritual.

A giant machine without its governor would tear itself apart, and would be utterly destroyed because it failed to obey its own laws of momentum or gravity.

An intellectual giant who fails to comply with the laws of learning will become an idiot. A metaphysical student who fails to comply with or obey the instructions of spirit, the "law of God," will reverse their good and create evil. We are constantly following instructions to operate.

We depend entirely on obedience for our success or failure in the process of living.

Who to obey is the question. What to obey and what not to obey is also the question.

Paul said it this way in **Romans 6:16-18**: *"Know you not, that to whom you yield yourselves servants to obey, His servants you are to whom you obey; whether to sin unto death, or of obedience unto righteousness? But God be thanked, that you were the servants of sin,* *but you have obeyed from the heart the form of doctrine which was delivered you. Being then free from sin, you became the servants of righteousness."*

We must learn to obey the spirit within us instead of the conditions about us.

Let's look at obedience from another point of view than we usually do.

Let's look at it from a higher-level point of view.

The Bible tells us in **Deuteronomy 11:25-28** *"Behold* (look at this*), is set before you this day a blessing and a curse; a blessing, if you obey the commandments of the Lord your God, which I command you this day; and a curse, if you will not obey the commandments of the Lord, your God, but turn aside out of the way which I command you this day to go after other gods, which you have known."*

Other gods. Your car, house, stocks, bonds, insurance, husband, wife, children, job, clothes, whatever you put before love more, honor more, than God and His word.

Isaiah 1:19-20 *"If you are willing and obedient, you shall eat the good of the land; but if you refuse and rebel, you shall be devoured with the sword; for the mouth of the Lord has spoken."*

When we obey God we must be obeyed!

What do you mean by that, Rev. Della?

By obeying the word of God, Jesus was able to calm the raging sea. It had to obey Him and be still.

By obeying the word of God, you too are able to

calm the raging seas of your life, world and affairs.

Matthew 8:25-27 *"His disciples awoke Him saying 'Save us we perish.'*

He said to them, 'Why are you fearful, o ye of little faith.' Then He rose and rebuked the winds and the sea; and there was a great calm.

And the men marveled saying what manner of man is this, that even the winds and the sea obey Him?"

Mark 1:27 *"And they were all amazed in so much that they questioned among themselves, saying, 'What thing is this; what new doctrine is this? For with authority commandeth He even the unclean spirits, and they do obey Him.'"*

By obeying the word of God, Jesus was able to command the unclean spirits to leave and they had to obey and leave.

By obeying God, we too can make the unclean spirits in our lives obey us.

They put Peter and the Apostles in jail, for preaching and teaching the Gospel.

The doors of prison were opened for Peter and the other Apostles and God told them, *"Go stand in the temple and speak to the people all the words of this life."*

Now they had just gotten out of prison. They were in there in the first place for preaching to these same people, now the Father was telling them to preach and teach them again.

Acts 5:28-29, 32. The police came and said to Peter and the Apostles, *"Did not we strictly command you that you should not teach in this name? And behold, you*

*have filled Jerusalem with your doctrine, and intend to
bring this man's blood upon us.*

*Then Peter and the other Apostles said, 'We ought
to obey God rather than men. And we are His witnesses
of these things, and so is also the Holy Ghost, whom God
has given to they that obey Him.'"*

We must obey the Lord for revelation, right
direction, love, peace, joy, prosperity, health, strength and
the correct use of all our faculties.

When we do, the whole spirit of God, which is
God in action, will find what we need and bring it to us or
lead us to it. All of God's instructions are for our success
and life more abundantly. He will never make you do
anything, because He has given you freedom of choice.

He wants us to decide of our own free will to obey
Him.

1 Samuel 15:22 *"Has the Lord as great delight in
burnt offerings and sacrifices, as in obeying the voice of
the Lord; behold to obey is better than sacrifice."*

2 Corinthians 2:9 Paul says, *"For this end also
did I write, that I might know the proof of you, whether
you are obedient in all things."*

Are we obedient in all things?

We are most apt and able to be obedient in good
times but when things get sticky, we don't always realize
(see with our real eyes, our spiritual eyes) when fear and
anger attack do we obey and *"fear not?"*

Do we obey by judging the righteous judgment or
are we still being thrown off judging by appearances?

Do we ask in His name knowing that He will do

145

what we ask?

It is not easy; He never said it would be easy. He said it would be worth your while.

It wasn't easy for Jesus.

Matthew 26:39, 42 *"And He went a little farther, and He fell on His face and prayed, saying, 'O my Father, if it is possible let this cup pass from me; never the less, not as I will, but as You will.'*

And He went again the second time and prayed saying, 'O, my Father, if this cup may not pass away from me, except I drink it, thy will be done.'"

Are we as Christian followers of Christ, willing to submit our will to God's will and forgive seventy times seven or do we feel we have to hold a grudge?

Do you love yourself enough to have a pattern worthy of loving your neighbor as you love yourself?

Do we obey *"freely you have received, freely also give"*?

Are we obeying by being a blessing or are we being a disaster looking for a place to happen?

In sickness or disease are you obeying by using your brain or are you busy petting the pain?

Are you obeying by putting your hand to the plow and never looking back or are you playing those old mental tapes over and over?

Are you obeying by going to the secret place listening for the still small voice or are you giving your power to the pain and fear and seeming lack by talking about it constantly?

Are you willing to say, "Even though this cup is bitter and I must drink it, Father not my will but thy will be done? For I know Your will for me is absolute good"?

Jesus obeyed, and He was able to go through the cross, through the grave, through the resurrection to the ascension.

If you will obey, you too can go through whatever your cross is, even through the grave to the resurrection to the ascension.

Jesus speaking, "*If you keep my commandments* (if you will obey), *you shall abide in my love, even as I have kept my Father's commandments* (obeyed my Father) *and abide in His love, these things I have spoken unto you that my joy may remain in you and that your joy may be full.*" **John 15:10-11**

Joshua 24:15 "*Choose ye this day whom you will serve; but as for me and my house, we will serve the Lord.*"

It's your choice to make.

I obey my Father and I make no mental images of lack.

I speak no words of limitation.

I look only to God for the fulfillment of my desires and my needs.

You Can Have

As Far As You Can See

We say this and sing this every Sunday at Understanding Principles for Better Living Church. Now, we are going to get a little deeper into the meanings that are in this allegory.

God made a covenant with Abram in **Genesis 12:1-4**.

"Now the Lord said unto Abram, Get thee out of thy country from thy kindred and from thy Father's house, unto a land that I will shew thee; and I will make of you a great nation and I will bless thee and make thy name great; and thou shall be a blessing; and I will bless them that bless thee, and curse him that curseth thee; and in thee shall all families of the earth be blessed.

And Abram obeyed and departed and took his wife Sarai and his brother's son with him. Along with their substance and the souls they had gathered in Haran."

"Haran," symbolizes where the mind is strengthened, and is determined to go on toward fuller spiritual enlightenment and upliftment.

It says Abram obeyed but he didn't. He took his brother's son with him. Lot was Abram's favorite nephew.

It is not always the great disobediences; sometimes it is the small comfort disobediences that ensnare us.

Lot: represents the negative side of faith. When your faith expands in consciousness and you go into a new country, which is a new way of thinking, its old subjective aspects go with it and they expand also.

So Lot starts grumbling there is not enough water, food, and land for his cattle and Abram's cattle so they couldn't dwell together.

Which may have been the only thing Lot ever said right.

And to prove his point, Lot created strife between them. They came close to fighting.

Abram said to Lot in **Genesis 13:8-10**, *"Let there be no strife, I pray thee between me and thee and my herdsmen and your herdsmen for we are brothers.*

Is not the whole land before us? Separate yourself, I pray from me.

If you will take the left hand, then I will depart to the right or if you depart to the right, I will go to the left.

Lot looked over and saw the plains of Jordan and it looked green and well watered and to be the best land and he chose that, not knowing it was Sodom and Gomorrah land that God would totally destroy."

Greed is not always gracious!

Land symbolizes your consciousness where ideas are planted and situations grown.

Land is creative soil out of which we create our experiences.

The land Lot chose were the experiences that followed him in Sodom and Gomorrah.

After Lot had gone, God made Abram a promise.

Genesis 13:14-16 *"And the Lord said to Abram, 'Lift up now your eyes and look from the place where you are--*

Northwest,--the conscious mind

Southwest,--the subconscious mind

Eastward,--within

and Westward,--outer appearances.

--for all the land which you see to you will I give it, and to thy seed forever.

And I will make thy seed as the dust of the earth so that if a man can number the dust of the earth, then shall thy seed also be numbered."

Seed symbolizes the creative idea inherent in the word.

The seed is a generative center through which intelligence (God) manipulates substance and produces form.

You will have so many ideas that they cannot be numbered because they are as many as grains of sand.

Genesis 13:17 *"Arise walk through the land in the*

length of it and the breadth of it, for I will give it to you".

Walk through your ideas, the length and breadth of those He has promised and will give you.

You can have as far as you can see!

When you look, what do you see?

Are you fooled by the green grass and "well watered" look, the appearances? Jesus told us not to judge by appearances. Appearances disguised Sodom and Gomorrah.

When you look do you see that the truth of God is always reliable?

Do you see you can make it better when you leave all your negative kindred behind, all your negative thoughts and actions, if you want to go into a new country in peace and prosperity?

Do you see from the peace that surpasses all human understanding or from the wars you choose to fight every day?

You can have as far as you see.

Do you see love or hate?

Do you see lack and limitation or do you see prosperity and opulence?

Do you see Jesus as your savior and protector and God as your loving Father? Or do you see the world and life able to and therefore is taking advantage of you?

Do you see with or from the old mental tapes that are filled with hate and hurt, fear, distrust, abuse, misunderstanding and confusion? Or do you see from

Jesus' instructions to love your enemies and your neighbors?

You can have as far as you can see.

Do you see plenty or not enough? Victory or defeat?

Do you see you with a way out or do you see you locked in a trap?

Do you see evil everywhere you look or do you see the Christ, at least in the people you know and say you love?

You need to see the truth from the north, which is your conscious mind.

You need to see it from the south, which is your subconscious mind.

You need to see it from the east, which is from the Christ within you.

And you need to see it from the west, which are your outer experiences.

Do you view things with a cynical critical eye for what you call self-defense? Or are you leaning on the everlasting arm, entrenched in your belief of and trust in God.

Belief = the mental act, condition, or habit of placing trust or confidence in a person or thing = Faith.

Abram had faith enough to become Abraham and to trust God's word that he could have as far as he could see. Because he believed God would do what He said He would, God responded by giving him, as far as he could see.

Abram not only did as God said but when he found out he was mistaken in bringing Lot, he peacefully said take whatever you want! God gave me this and He'll give me whatever I need, to make whatever you leave prosperous.

Where do you stand? And what do you see from where you stand?

Are you even looking at all? You cannot see it if you are not even looking. You cannot have it if you cannot see it. But glory be to God you can have as far as you can see, so you better start looking.

God is the source of my supply, and God provides His own channels of supply for me right now.

Thank you Father for Your unspeakable gifts.

Thank you that I am enriched in every phase of my life.

Thank you that it is Your promise and Your purpose that I should have as far as I can see.

My God Given Attitude

My God given attitude is:

I am Power for Success.

Because of my intense longings for God, I hunger and thirst after Him.

I am Power in a positive way,

Because my attitude is that my spirit is poor, in the spirit of selfishness,

And my personal consciousness is rich in the spirit of Christ.

Because Of My Attitudes

I am Health, I am Strength, I am Peace, because I am a Peace Maker,

And the Peace in me gives Peace to others.

I am Happiness; I am Prosperity, because the kingdom of heaven is mine.

I am free; I am Eternally Youthful and Poised because of my attitudes.

I do not depend upon persons or conditions for my prosperity. God is the source of my supply, and God provides His own amazing channels of supply for me right now!

My prosperity now comes to me from expected and unexpected channels in expected and unexpected ways. From all points of the universe, rich supply comes to me. Right now, in a perfect way, in the name and the nature of Christ Jesus.

Thanks and praise to God because that's the way it is in my life, world and affairs.

I Know The Truth
Jesus Knew

I know the truth Jesus knew.

My father knows what I need before I even ask Him.

It is already done in the realm of spirit.

I will not be deceived by appearances!

I will judge the righteous judgment.

I do not depend upon persons or conditions for my prosperity. God is the source and my supply.

God supplies His own amazing channels to supply me now.

I have an inner consciousness for wealth and plenty always accompanies me because I look to God and He guides me.

I am power for success in a positive way and I have and use my spiritual force to keep it that way.

I will not worry about finances, or threats to my position in any form. I will not assume a penchant for failing, for I am made in the image likeness of God, and God cannot fail, therefore neither can I.

I will make no mental images of lack.

I will have no other God.

Psalm Of Prosperity
by Charles Fillmore

The Lord is my banker; my credit is good.

He maketh me to lie down in the consciousness of omnipresent abundance.

He giveth me the key to His strongbox.

He restoreth my faith in His riches;

He guideth me in the path of prosperity,

For His name's sake.

Yea though I walk in the very shadow of debt,

I shall fear no evil, for thou art with me;

Thy silver and thy gold, they secure me.

Thou preparest a way for me in the presence of

The collector;

Thou fillest my wallet with plenty;

My measure runneth over.

Surely goodness and plenty will follow me

all the days of my life,

And I shall do business in the name of the Lord

Forever.

Written in 1936

Made in the USA
Middletown, DE
25 May 2015